HIGHWAYS
INTO HISTORY

HIGHWAYS INTO HISTORY

Alice Fleming

St. Martin's Press New York

First Printing
Library of Congress Catalogue #70–145819
Manufactured in the United States of America

St. Martin's Press
175 Fifth Avenue
New York, N.Y. 10010

AFFILIATED PUBLISHERS: Macmillan & Company, Limited, London
—also at Bombay, Calcutta, Madras and Melbourne—the Macmillan
Company of Canada, Limited, Toronto.

Preface

Millions of highways crisscross the landscape of the United States. Most people think of them only as a convenient way to get from one place to another. They forget—or perhaps never knew—that many of these roads have colorful pasts.

N.Y. 5 was an ancient trail of the Iroquois Indians. U.S. 1 was the route taken by George Washington when he assumed command of the Continental Army at Cambridge, Massachusetts. U.S. 50 saw the birth and death of the Pony Express.

History has been made along highways and highways themselves have made history. They have been blazed by Spanish missionaries, British soldiers and American frontiersmen, traveled on by spies and scoundrels, poets, presidents and pioneers.

The story of the nation's roads is the story of its growth. It can best be told by looking beyond the lines on the maps and the numbers on the signposts and following some of America's most famous highways into history.

Contents

Illustrations

I

U.S. 1 The Boston Post Road

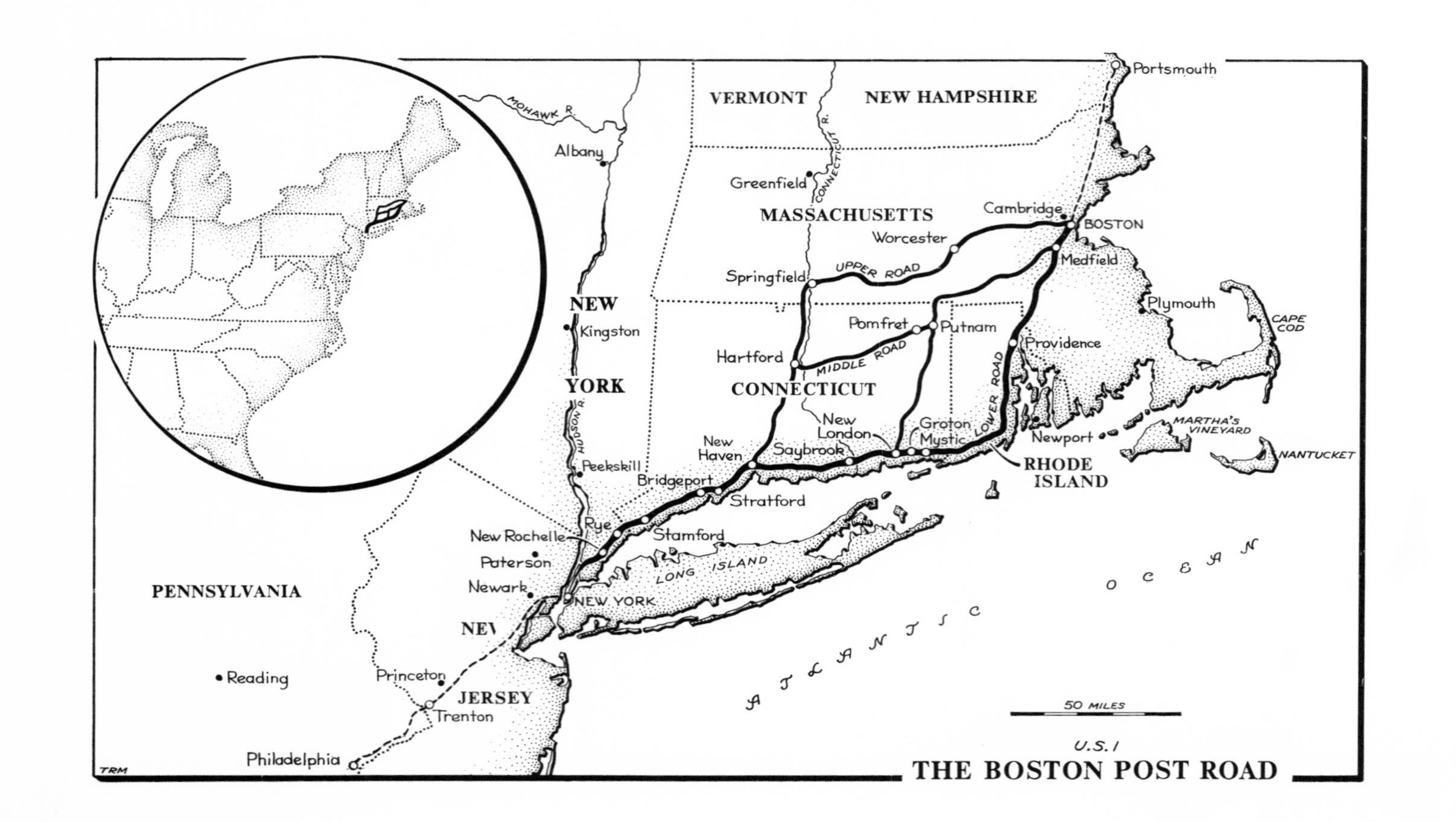

THE BOSTON POST ROAD

U.S. 1 is the oldest highway in the United States. It dates back to 1673 when a stouthearted post rider carried a packet of mail from New York to Boston.

No one knows the name of that first traveler on the primitive road through the wilderness. We know only that it took him two full weeks to make the journey. He found few inns and his only trail was one he mapped out for himself, using three already existing Indian paths through the woods.

In New York there was the Westchester Path which the Mohicans used to keep in touch with their neighbors in New England. In southern Connecticut the Pequot Path connected the villages on Long Island Sound, and in the northern part of the colony the Connecticut Path was a link between Boston and the parts of Massachusetts around the Connecticut River Valley.

The early colonists called the Indian trails "trodden paths." At first they were barely visible, but as the white men in their heavy boots started using them, the paths gradually became more clearly defined. They grew wider when the colonists began carrying their goods on pack horses and wider still when wagons were used. These crude pathways were the only roads of any length in the American colonies.

According to law, all able-bodied men between the ages of sixteen and sixty had to work one day a year on the town streets and another day on the King's Highway or Great Road—the larger thoroughfare that connected one town with another. The men were usually quite willing to clear the "ways" between the center of the village and the outlying houses and farms, but few of them felt any responsibility for the Great Road. In most cases, they cleared a path to the edge of town and stopped.

It's hard to say how long the King's Highway in the colonies might have remained blocked by trees and boulders had not the King himself, Charles II, started to worry about keeping his American subjects in closer touch with each other. In 1672 King Charles wrote to Francis Lovelace, his Royal Governor in New York, about the problem. Lovelace, in turn, consulted with Connecticut's governor, John Winthrop. The two men agreed that the best way to maintain contact among the King's subjects was to organize a postal system between New York and the New England colonies of Connecticut and Massachusetts.

The plan was to hire a man who would set out from New York on the first Monday of the month and return from Boston some time within the same month. The rider would carry "letters and other such portable packes" and must not only be "sworne as to his fidelity" but must also be "active, stout and indefatigable." No one else could have survived the journey.

The post rider's path took him across swift rivers, up and down rocky hillsides and through forests inhabited by wolves and bears. The towns along the way, although they have since grown into sizeable cities, consisted then of little more than a church, a couple of houses and a few farms.

The route started from Fort James at the tip of Manhattan Island up to the village of New Harlem. From there the post rider crossed the Harlem River at Spuyten Duyvil, took the Westchester Path east to the shores of Long Island Sound and then followed the Pequot Path as far as New Haven. At New Haven, he turned north toward Hartford and Springfield and then east again across the Connecticut Path through Worcester to Boston.

This first post road to Boston was soon known as the Upper Road. Later two alternate routes were established from New Haven. One, the Middle Road, went as far as Hartford, then turned off and headed through Pomfret and Putnam, Connecticut, and Uxbridge and Medfield, Massachusetts. The other, the

Lower Road, is the present U.S. 1. It runs parallel to Long Island Sound as far as Old Saybrook and New London, Connecticut, then continues up to Providence, Rhode Island, and on to Boston.

The first post rider left New York in January 1673, and despite the lack of an adequate road managed to get to Boston and back within a month as Governor Lovelace had specified. The service came to an abrupt halt the following August when a fleet of twenty-three Dutch warships sailed into New York Harbor.

An English fleet had captured the city from the Dutch nine years before. Now its former owners demanded its return. When the vessels opened fire on Fort James, the English quickly surrendered and New York again became New Amsterdam. This time the Dutch held the city only six months. On February 19, 1674, they signed the Treaty of Westminster, which made it an English colony once more.

The postal service did not resume because by then, King Philip, sachem of the Wampanoag Indians, had declared war on the white settlers, and most of the warriors in New England were on the warpath.

Angry because the Englishmen were taking his people's lands and trying to make them obey English laws, Philip ordered his braves to burn a number of villages in Massachusetts and Rhode Island. The white men decided to retaliate and on December 19, 1675, over 1000 soldiers from the colonies of Massachusetts Bay, Plymouth and Connecticut marched against the Indians.

The Narragansetts, who were allies of the Wampanoags, had fortified an island in the middle of a swamp not far from U.S. 1 near the present town of West Kingston, Rhode Island. The colonists attacked it, killing hundreds of Indians, including women and children, burning their wigwams and destroying their supplies of food. Although the war did not end until King Philip was shot the following August, the Great Swamp Fight was a major defeat for the Indians. Soon after that the New England tribes gave up their lands and began moving to Canada and the west.

For many years after King Philip's War, there was little traffic between New York and Boston. Then in 1692 the English monarchs, William and Mary, decided to reinstate the postal service, and a Scotchman from New Jersey, Andrew Hamilton, was put in charge.

Hamilton's plans were more ambitious than Governor Lovelace's had been. The new mail route was to go beyond Boston to Portsmouth, New Hampshire, and from New York it would extend south to Philadelphia and Baltimore. Instead of the original once-a-month schedule, the new post riders left every two weeks in winter and twice a week in summer.

With the increased traffic the post riders' route grew from a bridle path to a somewhat wider road; a few more inns appeared, but these were the sole improvements.

A Boston school teacher named Sarah Kemble Knight made a trip along the Post Road to New York in 1704. Like other early travelers on the route, she went by horseback with the post rider serving as her guide. The 250-mile journey took eight days and when Mrs. Knight returned home to Boston some months later, she wrote these lines:

> Through many toils and many frights
> I have returned, poor Sarah Knights
> Over great rocks and many stones
> God has preserved from fractured bones.

Hugh Finlay, a postal inspector, toured the Lower Road between New London and Providence almost seventy years later. He called it "bad past all conceptions." But by that time, thanks to Benjamin Franklin, the road at least boasted milestones.

In 1751 Franklin had been appointed to Andrew Hamilton's former post as Deputy Postmaster for His Majesty's Provinces. Franklin established a system of postal routes, selecting the fastest roads and the safest ferry crossings. His biggest problem, however, was the postal rates. Charges were supposed to be made on the basis of how many miles a letter was sent, but since no one knew the precise distance from one town to another, there were constant arguments over the price.

The Wayside Inn, at South Sudbury, Massachusetts, perhaps the most famous of the many inns and taverns that lined the Boston Post Road during colonial days.

Ben Franklin finally decided to settle the matter once and for all. He made a 10-week trip through New England, riding up and down the Upper, Middle and Lower Post Roads with a special attachment on the wheels of his carriage to measure each mile he traveled. The miles—about 500 in all—were then marked off with stones that were set along the roadway by a team of workmen who followed Franklin's carriage. The milestones not only solved the problem of postal rates, they also improved the roads' appearance and served as good locations for inns and taverns.

Benjamin Franklin made many trips along the future U.S. 1 in the course of his duties as Deputy Postmaster. When he had the opportunity, he stopped for a few weeks' visit with his good friend Jared Eliot, a distinguished physician, who lived in Killingworth, now Clinton, Connecticut.

Early travelers along the Boston Post Road usually went by horseback and accompanied the mail rider, but after 1772 this was no longer necessary. Stagecoaches began to carry both mail and passengers between Boston and New York. The first stages were no more than boxes mounted on springs. They had four seats and could carry eleven passengers and the driver. For protection against the weather there was a top made of canvas or leather with curtains on the side that could be raised or lowered as the passengers wished. The seating was first come, first served, and since there were no side entrances, latecomers had to climb over the early arrivals and squeeze into whatever places they could find.

The Upper, Middle and Lower Post Roads became an important line of communication between Massachusetts and the other colonies during the tense days before the American Revolution. Some years before his celebrated midnight ride, Paul Revere thundered out of Boston and down the Post Road with dispatches from the Committees of Correspondence in Massachusetts to the other Committees in New York and Pennsylvania. The news of the Boston Massacre and the Boston Tea Party was also carried along the Post Roads, and a Stratford, Connecticut, post rider, Ebenezer Hurd, is supposed to have been the first to ride into New York with the story of the fighting at Lexington and Concord.

Several of the towns along the Lower Post Road were attacked and burned by British raiding parties who sailed across the sound from Long Island. After the war Connecticut bought 500,000 acres in Ohio and divided it among the citizens of the "suffering towns" to reimburse them for their losses. The New Englanders founded new villages, but they named them after the towns they had known in Connecticut—Greenwich, Norwalk, Fairfield, New Haven, New London and Groton.

The Revolution brought long-distance traffic on the Boston Post Road to a standstill. New York City was occupied by the British, and Westchester County became the neutral ground between the Tory armies in New York and the American patriots in neighboring New England. The Westchester Path was soon almost completely deserted.

Timothy Dwight, who was later president of Yale College, described the road in a book he wrote called *Travels in New York and New England.* "Where I had heretofore seen a continual succession of horses and carriages. . . ." he said, "not a single solitary traveller was visible from week to week or from month to month. . . . the very tracks of the carriages were grown over and obliterated. . . ."

Stagecoach travel resumed after the war, but for a while it looked as if boats might become the main system of transportation between New York and New England. A fleet of packet-sloops made regular trips on Long Island Sound, sailing from New York to Providence in as little as three days. From there it was only another day's journey overland to Boston.

The boats were at the mercy of the winds and tides, however, and on a bad run the trip could stretch from three days to nine or ten. Passengers who did not want to risk a delay, along with those who were prone to seasickness, were content to endure a week of the rocks and ruts of the old Boston Road.

A man who made the trip in 1785 lists some of the other inconveniences they had to contend with:

"The carriages were old and shackling and much of the harness was made of ropes. One pair of horses carried the stage eighteen miles. We generally reached our resting place for the night, if no accident intervened, at ten o'clock and after a frugal supper went to bed with a notice that we should be called at three the next morning, which generally proved to be half past two.

"Then, whether it snowed or rained, the traveller must rise and make ready by the help of a horn lantern and a farthing candle and proceed on his way over bad roads, sometimes with a driver showing no doubtful symptoms of drunkenness which good-hearted passengers never fail to improve at every stopping place by urging upon him another glass of toddy.

"Thus we travelled eighteen miles a stage, sometimes obliged to get out and help the coachman lift the coach out of a quagmire or rut, and arrived at New York after a week's hard travelling, wondering at the ease as well as the expedition of our journey."

Some years after the Revolutionary War ended, the Boston Post Road played host to a distinguished traveler—George Washington, the newly elected President of the United States. Washington had first journeyed along the Boston Post Road in 1775 when he rode from Philadelphia to Cambridge to become Commander-in-Chief of the Revolutionary Army. His later trip as President was part of an inaugural tour of the entire country.

George Washington's visit to "the Eastern states" took place in the fall of 1789. He started from New York, then the nation's capital, and traveled through a series of quiet country towns that are now the suburban New York communities of Eastchester, New Rochelle, Mamaroneck and Rye. In Rye he stayed at a tavern that was run by a widow named Haviland. Washington described it in his journal as "a very neat and decent Inn." The trim white building, which is also known as the Square House, is still a landmark in the town of Rye.

The President purposely omitted Rhode Island from his itinerary because that state had yet to ratify the Constitution. When it did, in the spring of 1790, Washington promptly arranged for a trip along the Lower Post Road and brief visits to Newport and Providence.

Most of the towns that Washington journeyed through were

old even in 1790. New Haven was settled in 1638 and had already earned a place in history as the refuge of the two judges, Edward Whalley and William Goffe, who had ordered the English King Charles I beheaded. When Charles's son, Charles II, took the throne in 1660, the judges were forced to flee. The King's soldiers followed them to Connecticut, but the judges escaped by hiding in a cave in what is now West Rock Park in New Haven.

Today New Haven is better known as the site of Yale University, a school that had its beginnings in several other towns along U.S. 1. It was founded in Branford in 1701 when ten Congregational ministers, each with a donation of books, met at the Reverend Samuel Russel's home to organize the "Collegiate School within his Majesties Colony of Connecticot."

The first classes were held at the Reverend Abraham Pierson's house in nearby Killingworth, now Clinton. After Pierson's death in 1707 the school was moved to Old Saybrook where it remained until 1716, when it finally was moved to New Haven.

The Revolutionary War spy, Nathan Hale, graduated from Yale in 1773 and taught school in another Lower Post Road city, New London. Today New London is famous as the site of the U.S. Navy's submarine base and as the home of the Coast Guard Academy; but the city's seafaring tradition dates back to the days of New England's clipper ships.

The era of the sailing ships is very much alive further along the Post Road at Mystic Seaport, where visitors can study various exhibits of maritime history and board the whaling ship *Charles W. Morgan* and the old three-masted ship *Joseph Conrad.*

Providence, Rhode Island, another old port along U.S. 1, has streets with names like Africa, Packet and Canton. Others are called Friendship, Hope and Benevolent, names given to them by Roger Williams, the clergyman who founded the Rhode Island Colony in 1636.

Of the many travelers along the Post Road, few were welcomed as enthusiastically as the Marquis de Lafayette. Lafayette had joined the Continental Army in 1777 and had served with distinction in several campaigns, including the final victory at Yorktown. The Americans had taken the 19-year-old French nobleman to their hearts and had made his name a symbol of the friendship between France and the United States.

As a gesture of the nation's continuing gratitude, President James Monroe invited Lafayette to return to America. The former officer, now sixty-seven, agreed and in 1824 made a triumphal tour of the country. In the course of his sixteen months' stay in America, Lafayette made two trips through New England.

He was in Boston in the summer of 1825 and celebrated the fiftieth anniversary of the Battle of Bunker Hill by laying the cornerstone for the Bunker Hill Monument.

By the time Lafayette made his tour of New England, most sections of the road between Boston and New York had been improved by turnpikes. Turnpikes were not a new idea. They had originated in medieval England. At that time, a turnpike was a metal bar that was inserted into a gate to keep people from entering a road until they paid a toll. By the time the word reached New England several hundred years later, it had come to mean the toll road itself rather than the barrier across it.

Between 1792 and 1810 more than 150 turnpike companies were chartered in New England. The companies were granted authority over a stretch of road anywhere from three to fifty miles long. They were supposed to clear away trees and boulders, drain swampy areas and otherwise keep the roads in passable condition. In return they could erect gates at various points along the highway and charge tolls ranging anywhere from twenty-five cents for a four-wheeled carriage drawn by two horses to three cents a dozen for a herd of pigs.

The only travelers who were excused from paying tolls were people traveling on the Lord's Day, those going to church, meetings or funerals, town residents going back and forth to their farms or to the local grist mill, and militiamen on their way to military exercises and reviews.

Tolls were not paid cheerfully anywhere along the old pikes, but the thrifty New Englanders particularly resented the road companies' assaults on their pocketbooks. When it became known that the gatekeeper in Old Saybrook, Connecticut, was in the habit of retiring early, travelers simply waited until the lights went off in the toll house. The turnpike company eventually solved the problem by allowing the man to keep any tolls he collected after nine o'clock at night. The gatekeeper promptly became a night owl and anyone who wanted to slip past the toll gate had to stay up until after midnight to do it.

Hordes of other resentful Yankees outwitted the turnpike companies by bypassing the main road and opening up smaller roads, called shunpikes, which managed to skirt the tollgates. Similar shunpikes are still in use to avoid tolls on the modern New England Thruway.

The early stagecoaches on the Boston Road were slow, lumbering vehicles that took almost a week to make the trip. Eventually, they were replaced by lighter, more comfortable coaches made by a pair of carriage makers in Concord, New Hampshire, Stephen Abbot and Lewis Downing. The Concord coaches were the same as the ones that were later used in the west, but the eastern stages were never held up by bandits—not because easterners were any more honest than westerners, but because New York and New England merchants dealt in hard-to-cash checks and bank drafts rather than silver dollars.

The first Concord coaches started operating around 1826. Their lighter weight made them much swifter than the earlier models and by then the road had been improved as well. Before long the trip between Boston and New York was reduced to an amazingly swift twenty-four hours. To celebrate the historic breakthrough, bonfires were lighted by the roadside and bells were rung in all the churches along the way.

The era of the New England stagecoach lasted until about 1840 when the railroad and the steamship took over; but with the

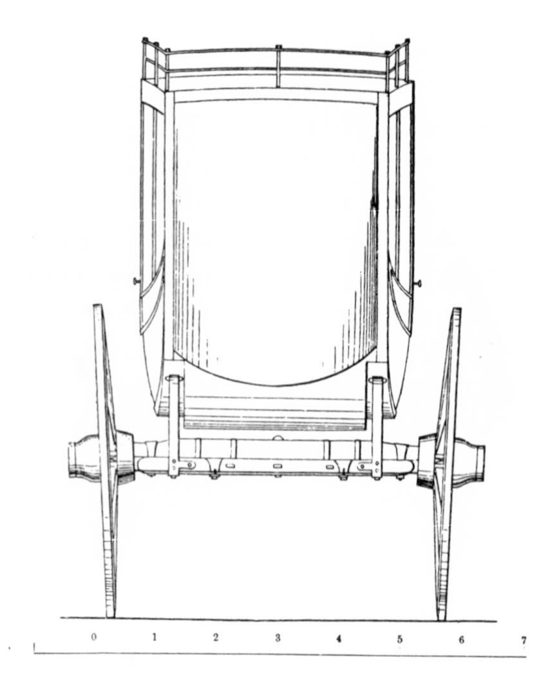

The Concord Coach. (Courtesy Wells Fargo Bank)

advent of the automobile in the twentieth century, the Lower Post Road again became an important highway.

Today a highspeed thruway, Interstate 95, covers the same general route as U.S. 1, but the nation's first highway has by no means been abandoned. It is still a link between most of the major cities on the eastern seaboard. Even though its milestones and stagecoach stops have been replaced by traffic lights and hamburger stands, its history is still alive for anyone who takes the time to look for it.

2

U.S. 25 The Wilderness Road

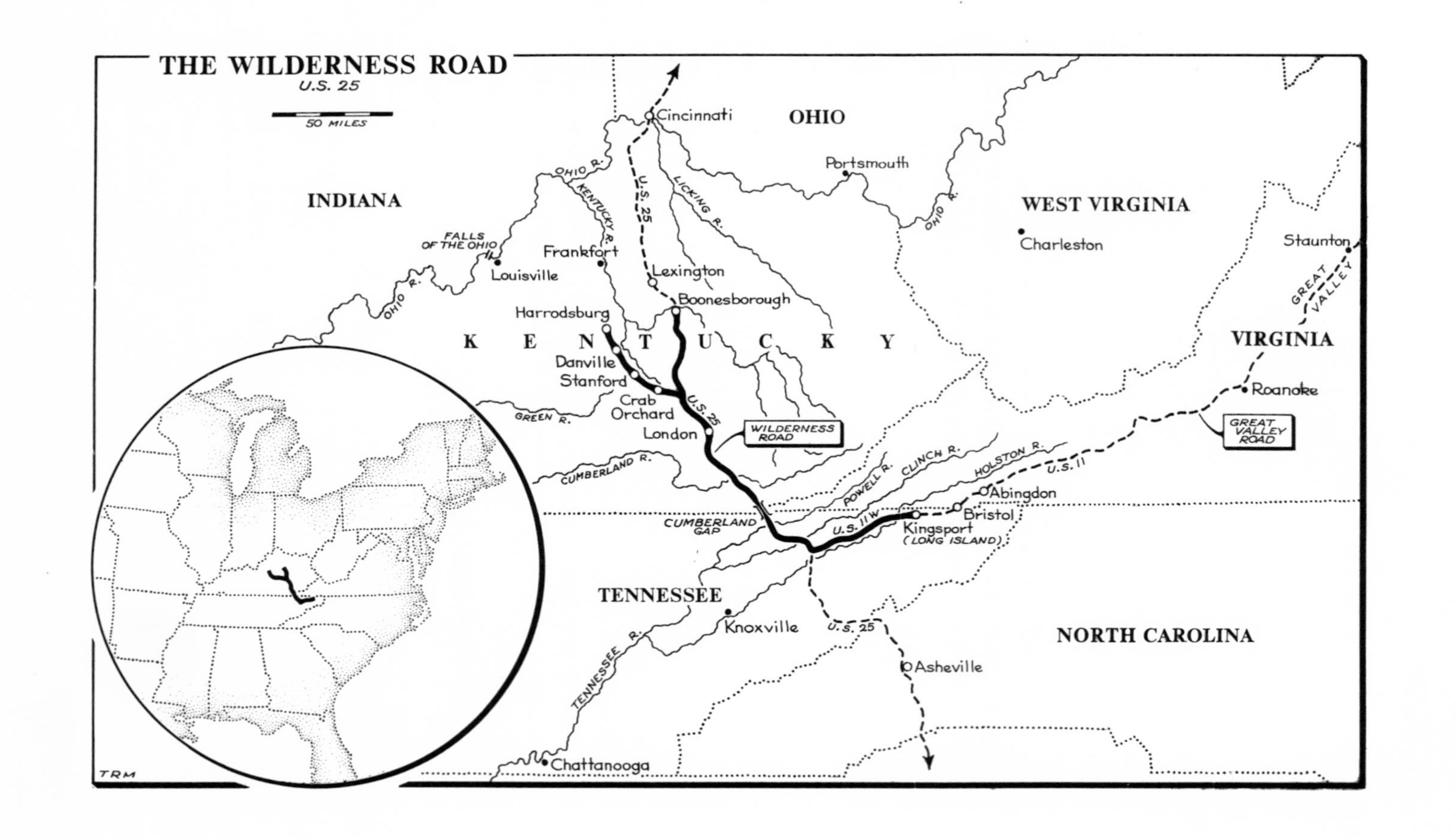
THE WILDERNESS ROAD
U.S. 25
50 MILES
INDIANA
OHIO
WEST VIRGINIA
VIRGINIA
KENTUCKY
TENNESSEE
NORTH CAROLINA
Cincinnati
Portsmouth
Charleston
Staunton
Roanoke
Frankfort
Louisville
Lexington
Boonesborough
Harrodsburg
Danville
Stanford
Crab Orchard
London
Abingdon
Bristol
Kingsport
(LONG ISLAND)
Knoxville
Asheville
Chattanooga
FALLS OF THE OHIO
OHIO R.
KENTUCKY R.
LICKING R.
GREEN R.
CUMBERLAND R.
POWELL R.
CLINCH R.
HOLSTON R.
TENNESSEE R.
CUMBERLAND GAP
U.S. 25
U.S. 11
U.S. 11 W
WILDERNESS ROAD
GREAT VALLEY ROAD
GREAT VALLEY
TRM

U.S. 25, the Dixie Highway, runs from Greenville, South Carolina, to Detroit, Michigan, but its oldest and most interesting section is in Kentucky where it follows the route of America's first highway to the west—the Wilderness Road.

The United States began as a string of small colonies on a narrow strip of land along the Atlantic seaboard. The strip quickly grew wider as more settlers came and pushed their way back from the shoreline, but in Virginia it stopped abruptly about 150 miles inland. There a series of steep mountain ranges, part of the craggy Appalachian chain, formed a natural barrier to the lands beyond.

The first white man to find a break in this seemingly impassable wall was a Virginia explorer named Thomas Walker. Walker had studied medicine at the College of William and Mary, but he gave up his practice in Fredericksburg to join a group of speculators who were exploring southwestern Virginia with an eye to investing in land. Walker made a number of expeditions through the Shenandoah Valley and into Tennessee. On one of them he discovered a narrow passage through the mountains. It led into a land that had been the scene of many Indian wars. The Indians called it *Ken-ta-ke*—meaning "dark and bloody ground."

The adventurous doctor noted the discovery of "Cave Gap" in an entry in his journal dated April 13, 1750. Later he gave the gap, the mountains it passed through, and the river he found on the other side, the name Cumberland after the Duke of Cumberland, the hero of a battle against the Scottish rebels six years before.

Today the Cumberland Gap is a popular tourist attraction, but until Dr. Thomas Walker stumbled upon it, no one except the Indians knew it existed. Walker and his party followed one of their trails, Warriors' Path, across the mountains and into what is now southeastern Kentucky. They camped near the Cumberland River, built the first log cabin in Kentucky and stayed for several weeks exploring the countryside.

The French and Indian War, which lasted from 1754 to 1763, put an end to any further exploration of the Cumberland Gap. When the war ended, a few frontiersmen from Virginia's Shenandoah Valley began following the Warriors' Path through the gap into Kentucky. They hunted deer and buffalo and because their expeditions took them great distances and kept them away from home for long periods of time, they called themselves Long Hunters.

The Long Hunters roamed over much of the same countryside that Dr. Thomas Walker had visited in southeastern Kentucky. They also ventured into the central part of the state and returned to tell of a rich meadowland where the grass was so green it looked almost blue. Their tales of Kentucky's fabulous Bluegrass region eventually reached the ears of a wiry, dark-haired woodsman named Daniel Boone. They inspired him to become one of Kentucky's pioneer settlers and to blaze the trail that would help make the territory a state.

Daniel Boone had been born in Pennsylvania, but after his marriage in 1756, he and his wife Rebeccah settled in North Carolina's Yadkin River Valley. The Boones had a small farm in a settlement named Buffalo Lick, but Daniel was restless there. For a while he talked of moving to Pensacola, Florida, but Rebeccah objected and the plan was dropped.

Then one day an old friend of Boone's showed up in the Yadkin River Valley. His name was John Findley and he and Boone had served together in General Braddock's army during the French and Indian War. Findley was now a peddler of pots and pans, but he had once been a Long Hunter and during their army days he had often talked to Boone about the remarkable Bluegrass country he had seen in Kentucky.

John Findley had no sooner appeared at the Boones' cabin door than Daniel Boone began plying him with questions about the land beyond the Cumberland Gap. Before long the two men were making plans to go on a long hunt across the Warriors' Path so Boone could see Kentucky for himself.

They left in the spring of 1769 and were gone for almost two years. Daniel Boone found Kentucky as beautiful as he had expected it to be. When he arrived back in Buffalo Lick, he could talk of nothing but returning to live there with Rebeccah and their children.

Boone enlisted the aid of another frontiersman, Captain William Russell, and together they persuaded several other families —about forty people in all—to join them in the move. They set out for Kentucky in 1773, but they were barely past the Cumberland Gap when their camp was attacked by Indians. Six of the pioneers were killed, including Boone's 17-year-old son James. Although Boone was still eager to continue the journey, Russell and the others voted to return to Buffalo Lick as quickly as possible.

Daniel Boone made his next journey through the Cumberland Gap alone. A year after his disastrous attempt to move his family to Kentucky there was an Indian uprising known as Lord Dunmore's War. Boone was sent into Kentucky to warn the handful of men who had trading posts there to fortify their settlements and prepare for Indian attacks. He completed his mission in two months, traveling through eight hundred miles of wilderness infested with snakes, wolves, bears and Indians on the warpath.

Lord Dunmore's War ended in the fall of 1774 and with the Indians subdued, the way was again open for a settlement in Kentucky. By now Richard Henderson, a judge of the Superior Court of North Carolina, had become interested in the lands there. Henderson organized the Transylvania Company and in 1775 negotiated the Treaty of Sycamore Shoals with the Cherokee Indians. For the sum of ten thousand English pounds, the

Daniel Boone. (The Bettmann Archive)

Cherokees gave Henderson title to some twenty million acres between the Kentucky and Cumberland Rivers, comprising about half of the present state of Kentucky.

Passing through the Cumberland Gap. (Culver Pictures)

Henderson planned to resell the land to settlers, but before he could hope to interest anyone in his newly acquired property, he knew he would have to provide a road to get them there. He promptly hired Daniel Boone to widen the Warriors' Path through the Cumberland Gap and blaze a trail into Kentucky.

The Wilderness Road, as Boone's Trail was called, started at the Long Island of the Holston River, now the city of Kingsport, Tennessee. From there, Boone, with a band of 30 axmen, cleared his way through thick cane and reed and sturdy trees and in a single month blazed 208 miles of trail. The woodsmen stopped at a spot on the Kentucky River and built a fort that they called Boonesborough. It was the second white settlement in the Bluegrass region. Harrodsburg, thirty miles to the west, had been founded by James Harrod and a party of surveyors a few months before.

The first traveler on Daniel Boone's new Wilderness Road was Judge Richard Henderson, who came to inspect the holdings of his Transylvania Company. He was followed by a steady stream of families eager to settle in Kentucky. Some of them came from Virginia; others from Pennsylvania or Maryland. They traveled south through the great valley between the Blue Ridge Mountains and the Shenandoahs and Alleghenies. The route was called the Great Wagon Road, the Valley Turnpike and occasionally the Irish Road because so many immigrants from Ireland traversed it. It ended near the Long Island of the Holston where the travelers then turned on to the Wilderness Road.

The original Wilderness Road only went as far as Boonesborough, but it was soon extended. One group of pioneers went beyond Daniel Boone's fort and founded a settlement which they called Lexington. They selected the name because they arrived there on a spring day in 1775 just after they had received the news of the fighting on the green at Lexington, Massachusetts.

A branch of the Wilderness Trail which is not part of U.S. 25 developed when some of Kentucky's settlers started a second path at the Hazel Patch just north of the town of London. It forked off to the northwest and led to the falls of the Ohio, near the present city of Louisville.

For years the last civilized point on this road was at a place called the Crab Orchard. Travelers usually assembled there and joined forces for the more difficult journey ahead. The companies, which left every two or three weeks, recruited their members through advertisements in the newspapers. A typical notice that appeared in 1788 read:

> NOTICE
>
> A large company will meet at the Crab Orchard the 19th of November in order to start the next day through the Wilderness. As it is very dangerous on account of the Indians, it is hoped each person will go well armed.

Armed or not, the companies were regularly attacked. When they were, Colonel William Whitley usually organized a party of riflemen and came to their rescue.

Whitley lived at Walnut Flat, about five miles west of the Crab Orchard. A fierce and fearless Irishman, he had bought some land along the west branch of the Wilderness Road and built himself a two-and-a-half-story mansion, the first brick house in the state of Kentucky.

Sportsman's Hill, as the house is called, still stands near the present town of Stanford. It was a wondrous sight in a region where the only buildings were forts and log cabins. Whitley emblazoned his initials in white brick over the front entrance. He ordered glass for the windows and had it brought by packhorses from the east. On the mantle over the fireplace he carved a line of dollar signs to indicate the money that was to be made in the new country.

Among the Colonel's other decorative touches were a staircase with thirteen steps in honor of the thirteen colonies and a harp on the newel post in memory of his Irish ancestry. The house boasted a ballroom, but as a concession to its location in the wilderness, there was also a secret cupboard on the stairlanding where the women and children could hide in case of an Indian attack.

Although Whitley's principal occupation was farming, he was also the self-appointed protector of the Kentucky frontier. In his many skirmishes with the Indians, he was injured only once when the tip of his nose was grazed by a bullet. At the age of sixty-four, however, he enlisted as a private in the War of 1812 and was finally killed in a battle against the British.

Judge Richard Henderson had hoped to be the sole authority in his private colony of Transylvania, but the independent Kentucky pioneers rebelled. In 1776 the backwoodsmen sent two delegates, George Rogers Clark and John Gabriel Jones, to Williamsburg to ask for the protection of the Virginia government. Virginia agreed and Kentucky was annexed to the state as its westernmost county.

Traffic along the Wilderness Road slowed to a standstill during the early years of the American Revolution. Indians, incited by the British, attacked every white settlement they could find. The Indian attacks subsided when George Rogers Clark, leading an army of volunteers from Kentucky and Virginia, captured three major British forts in the west.

By the time Cornwallis surrendered at Yorktown in 1783, over 12,000 settlers had come to Kentucky, most of them by way of the Wilderness Road. Less than ten years later, in 1792, Kentucky had over 200,000 citizens and was ready to become an independent state. The Wilderness Road, which had helped to make the county a state, now became more important than ever.

Kentucky's first governor, Isaac Shelby, made the road a mail route between the Cumberland Gap and his home town of Danville. The road was still no more than the packtrail blazed by Daniel Boone and there was no money in the treasury to improve it; but Shelby prevailed upon Kentucky's leading citizens to raise the money themselves. There were several substantial donations and Colonel William Whitley agreed to supply rations of bacon for the workmen.

A few years later when Kentucky's treasury was fatter, Shelby undertook some more ambitious improvements. He announced that the trail was to be converted into a road thirty feet wide and capable of withstanding wagon loads as heavy as a ton. When the governor advertised in the *Kentucky Gazette* for someone to supervise the work, he received the following letter from Daniel Boone:

> feburey the 11th 1796
>
> Sir
>
> after my Best Respts to your Excelancy and family I wish to inform you that I have sum intention of undertaking this New Rode that is to be Cut through the Wilderness and I think My Self intiteled to the ofer of the Bisness as I first Marked out that Rode in March 1775 and never Re'd anything for my trubel and Sepose I am No Statesman I am a Woodsman and think My Self as Capable of Marking and Cutting that Rode as any other man.

Governor Shelby had lived for a while at Boonesborough and knew Daniel Boone personally. Nevertheless, he gave the contract for the road to two other men whom he evidently considered more capable than the 62-year-old Boone.

The work was completed by the end of the year and Shelby's road commissioners, Joseph Crockett and James Knox, announced the fact in a notice that took up almost the entire front page of the *Kentucky Gazette.*

"THE WILDERNESS ROAD from Cumberland Gap to the settlements in Kentucky is now compleated," it said. "Waggons loaded with a ton weight, may pass with ease, with four good horses—Travellers will find no difficulty in procuring such necessaries as they stand in need of on the road; and the abundant crop now growing in Kentucky, will afford the emigrants a certainty of being supplied with every necessary of life on the most convenient terms."

The improvements authorized by Isaac Shelby included grading and widening the road between the Cumberland Gap and

Crab Orchard. Blockhouses were erected at strategic points along the way to provide travelers with a place to defend themselves against outlaws and Indians. To pay for the upkeep of the new road the Governor ordered a tollgate—the first in Kentucky—erected not far from the western end of the Cumberland Gap. For the first few months of its existence, it, too, was an armed blockhouse. Travelers objected so strenuously to paying for the use of the road that armed men had to be kept on duty to see that they complied with the law.

In the first years after the American Revolution, Kentucky was considered the west and the Wilderness Road was the only road that led there. By 1800, however, emigrants were beginning to travel on other routes and to settle in other territories. A few years later, rivers had become America's most important highways and Kentucky's main roads were the Mississippi, the Ohio and the Cumberland.

In another twenty-five years, Daniel Boone's road faded into just another wagon trail and the pass through the Cumberland Gap was used mainly by drovers taking their livestock across the mountains to markets in the east. The old Warriors' Path regained some of its importance during the Civil War when both the Union and Confederate forces fought to control it, but after the war it became only a picturesque path through the mountains.

Today the Cumberland Gap is on the site of a 20,000-acre National Historical Park. It offers magnificent views of three different states—Kentucky, Virginia and Tennessee. There are also remains of the fortifications that were erected during the Civil War as well as a two-mile stretch of Daniel Boone's original Wilderness Road.

Other reminders of Daniel Boone and the Wilderness Road can be found on or near the modern Dixie Highway. At Kingsport, Tennessee, a bronze tablet near the center of the town shows the direction Boone and his axmen took to get to Kentucky. South of Kingsport, one arm of the Dixie Highway, Route

25E passes through Bean Station. The town was named after the four Bean brothers, who erected a fort there in 1787. For years, it was an important stop on the way to the Cumberland Gap, and in 1813 a tavern was built there that became known as one of the better inns in the area: Andrew Jackson and James K. Polk and Henry Clay all stayed there when they took the Wilderness Trail on their way back and forth to Washington.

Clay, who was Speaker of the House of Representatives and a long-time member of the Senate, started his career as a lawyer in Lexington. His estate, Ashland, still stands along U.S. 25 on the city's outskirts. It was designed by Benjamin Latrobe, the architect of the United States Capitol building, and is named Ashland because it stands in a grove of ash trees.

Lexington was also the childhood home of Mary Todd Lincoln; Abraham Lincoln came to court her in the Todds' Georgian colonial home on West Main Street. Another lovely Georgian home, this one open to the public, is the Hunt Morgan House on North Mill Street. A Confederate general, John Hunt Morgan, once lived there. Morgan was captured by Union troops but later escaped. According to the legends, he headed straight for Lexington, galloped his horse through the front door of the house, waved to his mother and with Yankee troops in hot pursuit galloped out the back.

Originally only a single blockhouse, Lexington today is a busy community of nearly 100,000 people. It is in the heart of the 8,000-square-mile Bluegrass region, and is noted for the excellence of its horses, many of them descended from horses brought by pioneers from Maryland and Virginia who traveled along the Wilderness Road.

Route 25E joins U.S. 25 at Corbin, the same spot where Daniel Boone turned north to get to Boonesborough. A few miles from Corbin, the road passes through London, the site of Levi Jackson Wilderness Road State Park. In 1784 a company of forty people camped here for the night on the banks of little Laurel River. They were attacked by Indians and all but three of the party were killed or captured. The land was later given to a Revolutionary soldier, Levi Jackson, as a reward for his services in the Continental Army. Jackson's grandchildren donated the 815-acre property to the state of Kentucky as a memorial to all the brave pioneers who traveled on the Wilderness Road.

Daniel Boone's original settlement at Boonesborough has completely disappeared. The Daughters of the American Revolution has placed a marker on the site of the old fort, but the stockade itself is gone and no attempt has been made to rebuild it.

Harrodsburg, the first settlement in Kentucky, however, is not far from the Dixie Highway on U.S. 127. The modern town contains Old Fort Harrod State Park with a replica of the first Fort Harrod and the stockade and blockhouses that the pioneers built to defend it. There is a museum with exhibits of early cooking utensils, furniture and hunting equipment as well as the log cabin in which Abraham Lincoln's parents, early Kentucky settlers, were married on June 12, 1806. On summer evenings, a play, *The Legend of Daniel Boone,* is shown in an outdoor amphitheater.

Wherever you travel in the Bluegrass State, you can find memories of Daniel Boone and his Wilderness Road. Kentucky has never forgotten that it owes its existence to both of them.

3

U.S. 9 The Albany Post Road

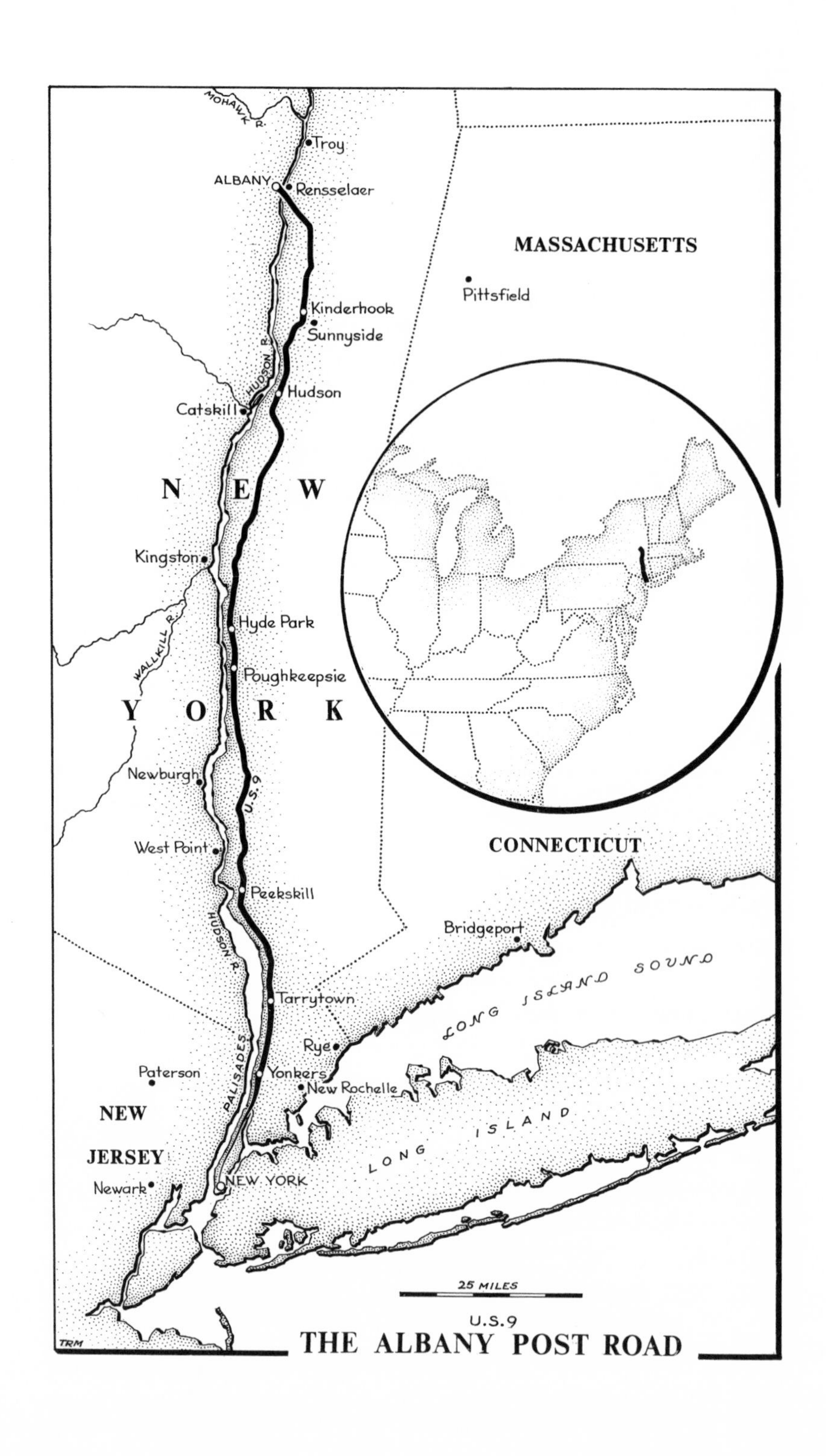

U.S.9
THE ALBANY POST ROAD

U.S. 9 might well be called the highway of famous Americans. Alexander Hamilton, John James Aubudon and Franklin D. Roosevelt owned houses along it; George Washington traveled on it; and Martin Van Buren and Washington Irving are buried beside it.

Once the main route connecting New York City and Albany, the old post road dates back to the earliest days of New York. Like so many of America's roads, it started as a series of Indian trails through the wilderness. Dutch settlers widened it and turned the path that ran through New Amsterdam into a wagon lane which they called DeHerre Straat, or Broadway.

The Englishmen who came after the Dutch broadened the road still further, and in 1703 the Provincial Legislature made the section between Kingsbridge—in what is now the Bronx—and Albany, a "Publick Highway." For a while it was called the Queen's Road in honor of England's ruler, Queen Anne. Later, when a post rider was engaged to carry the mail back and forth to Albany, the route became known as the Albany Post Road.

The first Dutch families arrived in New York in 1624. They built their settlements on the shores of the river that had been discovered and claimed for Holland by Henry Hudson. The first was Fort Orange, on the site of present-day Albany; the second was New Amsterdam. The two settlements thrived. Soon more Dutch colonists arrived to settle along the river banks, and the Hudson Valley became one of the most prosperous areas in the colonies.

In 1677 Stephanus Van Cortlandt bought 86,000 acres in the

valley near the mouth of the Croton River. The land was officially designated the Manor of Cortlandt and Stephanus became its First Lord. Another important property owner was Frederick Philipse. Philipse's estate started at Kingsbridge, opposite the northern tip of Manhattan Island, and stretched for twenty miles along the river, including the present cities of Yonkers and Tarrytown.

But the largest tract of all belonged to an Amsterdam diamond merchant, Kiliaen Van Rensselaer, who acquired 700,000 acres in the vicinity of Fort Orange. Van Rensselaer's holdings were almost 50 miles wide and extended 20 miles to the south along both sides of the Hudson.

U.S. 9 retains memories of these three pioneer land owners. Stephanus Van Cortlandt's sturdy manor house still stands along Route 9 in the town of Croton-on-Hudson and Frederick Philipse has left not one, but two, historic homes. The first, known as Philipse Castle, is in North Tarrytown. Philipse used the 24-room stone house as a residence when he toured the northern reaches of his vast estates, but he spent most of his time in his more pretentious Manor Hall, only a few yards from Route 9 in Yonkers.

The house, which dates back to the 1680's, has still another claim to fame. During the French and Indian War, a young lieutenant colonel in the Virginia Militia stopped off there while on his way to Boston to confer with his British commander-in-chief. The soldier's name was George Washington and according to the legends, he was in love with Frederick Philipse's great-great-granddaughter, Mary. Mary Philipse later married Washington's friend and fellow officer, Roger Morris. When the American Revolution began, she and her husband remained loyal to the King. Abandoning their extensive property in New York, they went to live in England.

There were several manor houses on Kiliaen Van Rensselaer's immense estate. The only one that remains is Fort Crailo in the Albany suburb of Rensselaer. The house is believed to have been built in 1704 by Kiliaen's younger brother Hendrik but the foundation was probably dug for an earlier fort that stood on the site. A stone in the cellar is inscribed "1642."

During the French and Indian War, Fort Crailo was the headquarters for the commander of the British forces in upper New York State, Major General James Abercrombie. There is a well in the backyard where, according to tradition, Abercrombie's regimental surgeon, Dr. Richard Shuckburgh, wrote the words to "Yankee Doodle." The doctor was inspired, so the story goes, by some bedraggled volunteers from Connecticut who joined the British regulars at Albany for the assault on Fort Ticonderoga.

One of the most dramatic episodes in the history of Route 9 occurred during the Revolutionary War. On September 21, 1780, three self-appointed American sentries, David Paulding, Isaac Van Wart and David Williams, encountered a lone horseman riding along near the outskirts of Tarrytown. The trio decided to search the stranger and discovered some papers concealed in his boot. They were plans, drawn up by the American commander at West Point, Benedict Arnold, for delivering the strategic fortress to the British.

The captured horseman proved to be an English officer, Major John André, who had sailed up the Hudson on a British warship for a secret conference with Arnold. The two met at a house on the opposite side of the river just south of West Point. André had planned to return to New York by boat, but the warship was frightened off by American artillery fire. He decided to exchange his uniform for a disguise, take the ferry across the Hudson and travel overland instead. The decision sealed his fate. Not only was he apprehended by the Americans, but because he was in disguise, he was sentenced to be executed as a spy.

André was hanged less than two weeks later at Tappan, New York. Although his body has since been removed to London's Westminster Abbey, the marker on his grave remains. It reads:

"His death, though according to the stern code of war, moved even his enemies to pity, and both armies mourned the fate of one so young and so brave. . . ."

The capture of Major André, as depicted in a 19th-century print. (Culver Pictures)

The whitewood tree under which Major André was captured is supposed to have been struck by lightning in 1801 on the very day that the infamous traitor, Benedict Arnold, died in England. The site, on the boundary line between Tarrytown and North Tarrytown, is now marked by a stone monument.

Route 9 played an earlier role in the American Revolution when Washington's troops fought a brief battle with the British at Harlem Heights. A plaque affixed to a wall on the Columbia University campus at Broadway and 116th Street commemorates the skirmish.

During the few weeks the American army remained on Manhattan Island, Washington made his headquarters in a white columned mansion that had belonged to his old friends Roger and Mary Phillipse Morris. The house, not far from Broadway at

Edgecombe Avenue and West 160th Street, is now known as the Jumel Mansion after one of its later owners, Madame Jumel, who married and later divorced Aaron Burr.

The Americans retreated from New York in October 1776. They did not return until November 25, 1783, when the last British forces evacuated the city and Washington rode triumphantly back into town. He is said to have spent the night before at a house along the Albany Road in the Bronx. It was owned by a descendant of Stephanus Van Cortlandt and stands in today's Van Cortlandt Park.

The first stagecoaches began running between New York and Albany soon after the American Revolution. The trip took three days and the fare was four pence a mile. Passengers were expected to pay for their own food and lodging along the way. A few of the inns they stopped at still survive. One, the Ferry House, is not far from Stephanus Van Cortlandt's manor house in Croton. Another, the Beekman Arms in Rhinebeck, dates back to 1700 and claims to be the oldest hotel in the country.

In 1807 the residents of the Hudson River Valley were astonished to see a strange-looking vessel gliding through the water without any sails. The boat, Robert Fulton's *Clermont,* was the first successful steamship. It marked the beginning of a new era in transportation and brought stage-coach traffic on the Post Road to an abrupt halt.

The steamboats were eventually superseded by railroads, and the trains by automobiles and planes, but in spite of these changes in our national travel habits, Route 9 has endured. It has been widened and paved, a few detours added and a few removed. Essentially, however, the road still follows the route of its post rider days.

For a long time the biggest detour on the Albany Post Road was in New York City. Broadway ended abruptly a few blocks above Cortlandt Street, so travelers had to veer east and follow the Boston Post Road to Kingsbridge. From there the Boston traffic continued eastward toward Long Island Sound while those bound for Albany headed north along the east bank of the Hudson River.

As New York grew, Broadway gradually pushed its way uptown. By 1824 it had reached 23rd Street and in another few decades it stretched to 59th Street. After that it became the Bloomingdale Road, a country lane that ran up the west side of Manhattan Island to Kingsbridge. Along the way it passed through Manhattanville, where Alexander Hamilton had built his handsome country house, The Grange, and Carmansville, where John James Audubon, the naturalist, had a home overlooking the river.

Hamilton's home was finished in 1802, but he lived in it for only two years. On July 11, 1804, he was mortally wounded in a duel with Aaron Burr. Audubon's home has long since disappeared, but The Grange is still standing. In 1889 it was moved to Convent Avenue and West 141st Street in Manhattan. Now in a sorry state of disrepair, it is expected to be moved again to the campus of the City University of New York and to be restored and refurnished by the National Park Service.

After the Civil War, Mayor William Marcy ("Boss") Tweed decided to pave the Bloomingdale Road and rename it the Western Boulevard. The corrupt boss was ousted from office before the job was finished and his proposed boulevard wasn't completed until the beginning of the twentieth century. By then the City Council had voted to call it Broadway. The longest street in New York, it now runs from the tip of Manhattan Island to the Yonkers city line.

As New York City's Broadway, U.S. 9 passes many points of interest. Best known, of course, is busy, brassy Times Square at Broadway and 42nd Street. Several dozen blocks south, at Wall Street, Trinity Churchyard contains the graves of Robert Fulton and Alexander Hamilton. At Fulton Street, one of Trinity's chapels, St. Paul's, is the church where President George Washington worshipped during his brief residence in New York, when the city was the nation's capital.

Farther uptown, the section around Broadway and 155th Street is the site of the once sleepy suburb of Carmansville. Trinity Church has another cemetery here. Among the famous New Yorkers who are buried in it are Madame Jumel, John James Audubon, and Clement Clarke Moore, author of the beloved poem "A Visit From Saint Nicholas." At the far end of Manhattan, the fieldstone and clapboard Dyckman house at Broadway and 204th Street has the distinction of being the only 18th-century farmhouse on Manhattan Island.

North of the Harlem River, which separates Manhattan from the Kingsbridge section of the Bronx, U.S. 9 follows almost the same route as the original highway to Albany. It passes through a succession of towns and cities whose names recall the days of the Indians, the Dutch and the English. Poughkeepsie comes from the Indians' *Apo-keep-sinck*—"a reed-covered lodge by the little water place." (If you have trouble spelling it, you may be relieved to know that local historians have discovered no less than forty-two different versions in the town's early records.)

Tarrytown, where Frederick Philipse's tenant farmers raised much of their grain, got its name from "tarwe", the Dutch word for wheat. Yonkers was originally owned by a man named Adriaen Van Der Donck. As the son of a gentleman, Van Der Donck merited the title *jonge heer* or "young lordship." His land became known as the Jonge Heer's land and eventually simply Yonkers.

The English left the names of two of their dukes in New York and Albany. They also christened Hastings after the battle where William the Conqueror won England in 1066, and Hyde Park after an early English governor of New York, Sir Edward Hyde.

The town of Dobbs Ferry took its name from Jeremiah Dobbs, an old Swede who operated a ferry across the Hudson in the latter part of the 17th century. Two hundred years later, the residents of Dobbs Ferry decided that its name wasn't dignified enough. They wanted to change it to something more impressive, something with a historic flavor.

When a meeting was called to discuss the matter, someone suggested renaming the town Paulding, after David Paulding, one of Major John André's captors who had lived in the area. Then another resident stood up and reminded the assembled citizens that Paulding had not been the only hero of the occasion. What about Isaac Van Wart? he asked with a perfectly straight face. The Van could be dropped and the town rechristened simply Wart-on-the-Hudson. The suggestion ended the discussion and Dobbs Ferry has remained Dobbs Ferry to this day.

Of the many prominent people who have lived in the Hudson River Valley, none has made it more famous than Washington Irving. Irving started his career as a lawyer, but gave up the law after the success of his *Knickerbocker's History of New York*. He traveled extensively abroad, but later returned to the United States and in 1835 bought an old Dutch farmhouse near Tarrytown that he transformed into a charming country villa much like the ones he had seen in Italy and France.

The house was called Sunnyside, and Irving once described it as "an old fashioned stone mansion all made up of gable ends and as full of angles and corners as an old cocked hat." It still stands by the side of U.S. 9 and contains most of the original furnishings and many of the author's personal belongings.

The early Dutch settlers called the bay above Tarrytown where the Hudson and Pocantico Rivers meet *Die Slapering Haven*. Washington Irving translated the phrase as Sleepy Hollow and made the area the scene of his famous "The Legend of Sleepy Hollow." The church that Ichabod Crane sang in is the same one that Frederick Philipse built for his tenants in 1697; the Headless Horseman is supposed to haunt its graveyard. The pretty heroine of the tale, Katrina Van Tassell, was modeled on a young lady named Helena Van Alen who lived farther along the old post road in the town of Kinderhook.

Washington Irving is buried in the graveyard of the Old Dutch Church. The millionaire steel manufacturer, Andrew Carnegie, rests there, too, as does William Rockefeller, brother and partner of the famous John D.

Washington Irving's Sunnyside, in Tarrytown, New York. (Courtesy Sleepy Hollow Restorations)

The oil magnate himself built a vast estate at Pocantico Hills, not far from Route 9. His grandsons and great grandsons still own houses on the property, and his son, the late John D. Rockefeller, Jr., was responsible for the restoration of such local landmarks as Sunnyside and the Van Cortlandt and Philipse Manor Houses.

As U.S. 9 wends its way northward, it passes through a number of important cities. Poughkeepsie, almost midway between New York and Albany, is the home of the college endowed by wealthy brewer Matthew Vassar. The city was the capital of New York for a brief period during the American Revolution. It is also famous as the place where the Smith brothers, William and Andrew, manufactured the world's first coughdrops, adding their bewhiskered faces as the trademark on every package.

Albany has been the capital of New York since 1797. One of the oldest communities in the 13 colonies, the city was founded in the early years of the 17th century and has been in continuous existence ever since. Its founders called it Fort Nassau; its first settlers changed the name to Fort Orange. After that it became Beverwyck and finally Albany.

U.S. 9 passes close to the State Capitol Building, a massive French chateau that was started in 1867 and took more than 30 years to complete. Three men who served as governor there—Grover Cleveland, Theodore Roosevelt and Franklin D. Roosevelt—went on to become Presidents of the United States.

Not far from the Capitol is the home of General Philip Schuyler, who served in both the French and Indian War and the American Revolution. In 1780, Schuyler's daughter, Elizabeth, was married in the parlor of the old mansion to a dashing young New Yorker named Alexander Hamilton.

President Martin Van Buren, who was born in Kinderhook, is buried in the town cemetery along Route 9. Kinderhook is often given credit for inspiring one of the most common expressions in the English language. When Martin Van Buren was running for the Presidency in 1836, his supporters nicknamed him Old Kinderhook, and shortened it to O.K. Everything that Van Buren stood for was labeled O.K. and the slogan was heard so often that it continued to be used even after the election was over.

Another United States President associated with U.S. 9 is Franklin Delano Roosevelt. The Roosevelt home in Hyde Park was bought by the President's father, James, in 1867. Franklin was born there on January 30, 1882. The original house dates back to 1826, but it has been remodeled extensively and a porch and colonnade added.

The town of Hyde Park was once only a railroad station for the great estates in the area, but FDR pushed it into world prominence. As President, he broadcast several of his famous fireside chats from his family home, and when King George VI and Queen Elizabeth of England visited the United States in 1936—the first time a British monarch set foot on American soil—the Roosevelts entertained them there. Mrs. Roosevelt made headlines when she invited the royal couple to a picnic and served a favorite American treat—hot dogs.

Today the Hyde Park house is a national historic shrine. The Franklin D. Roosevelt Library and Museum have been built on the grounds, and the President and his wife are buried in the Rose Garden.

Two miles north is the Frederick W. Vanderbilt estate. The house, which is open to the public, is a magnificent replica of an Italian Renaissance palace, decorated with priceless rugs, paintings and furniture.

Dozens of other wealthy Americans have lived along Route 9. Cyrus W. Field, who laid the first trans-Atlantic cable, had a house in Ardsley. Railroad tycoon and financier Jay Gould built a fantastic mansion, Lyndhurst, in Tarrytown. Sarah Breedlove Walker, a black businesswoman and philanthropist who made a fortune selling cosmetics, had an estate in Irvington, as did Alexander Hamilton's son James. The Hamilton house, Nevis, is now used as an atomic research laboratory by Columbia University.

One of the loveliest houses along the Hudson River is Boscobel, in Garrison. The mansion, whose name comes from the Italian, *bosco bello,* meaning beautiful woods, was built by States Morris Dyckman for his young wife, Elizabeth. Completed in 1806, it is a fine example of the architectural style developed by the Scottish designer Robert Adam.

The house fell into disrepair over the years, and in the 1950's it was scheduled to be demolished and a new building constructed on its site. A group of interested citizens raised enough money to dismantle the structure and move it piece by piece from its old

Boscobel

location on the Albany Post Road to a new one fifteen miles to the north on Route 9D.

Boscobel has since been completely restored, with much of its original china and silver returned. Now open to the public, the mansion has justly been called one of the most beautiful houses ever built in America.

With parkways and thruways connecting many of the cities along its route, the old Albany Road is no longer a major highway. Today it pokes lazily along through the Hudson River Valley, waking up to become Broadway or Main Street when it reaches a town. Sightseers who drive along it to visit Hyde Park or Sunnyside or stroll on it through Times Square or the financial district in New York City are often totally unaware that they are traveling on one of the most historic streets in the country.

4

NEW YORK 5 The Iroquois Trail

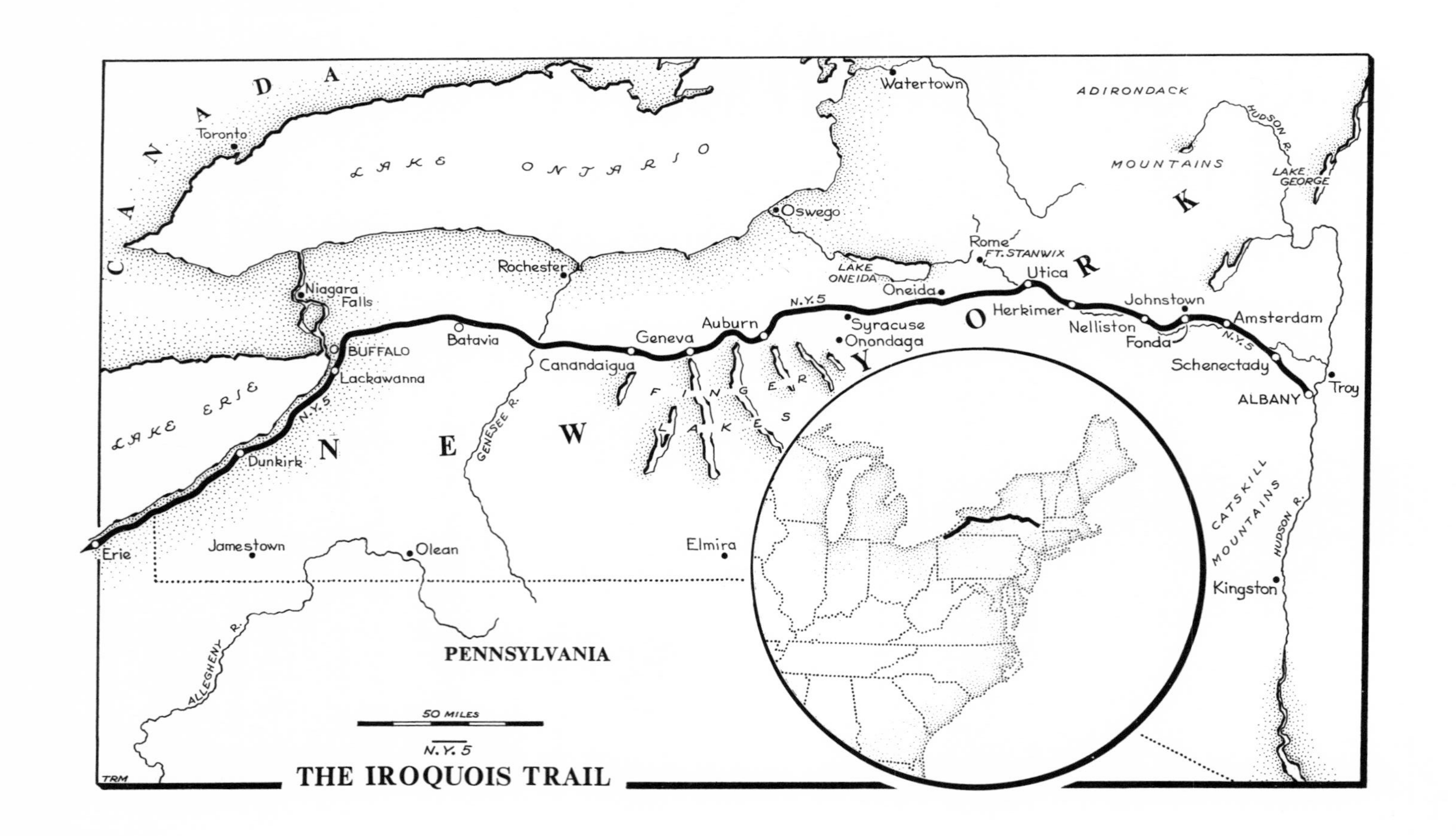

THE IROQUOIS TRAIL

Until the middle of the 17th century, most of the land in upper New York State belonged to the Iroquois Indians. They came from five different nations or tribes—the Mohawks, the Oneidas, the Onondagas, the Cayugas and the Senecas—and they had been organized into a confederation by the great Mohawk chief Hiawatha.

Each of the Five Nations had its own territory, and between the Long Houses, as they called their villages, ran a trail that reached from the Hudson River to Niagara Falls. The Iroquois used it when they were summoned to a Great Council Fire at Onondaga, the meeting place of the Five Nations. The Indians are gone now but Onondaga still exists near the city of Syracuse, and the Iroquois Trail survives as New York State Highway 5.

Route 5 begins at Albany—an appropriate beginning, since it was from the Dutch fort that the first white men set out to explore the wilderness to the west. The Mohawks, fiercest of the Five Nations, guarded the gateway to the Iroquois lands, but they were surprisingly cordial to the strangers who visited their Long Houses. They invited them to share their campfires and agreed to give them deer hides and beaver skins in exchange for blankets, steel traps and guns.

The Mohawks were less eager to welcome settlers who would clear the land and destroy their hunting grounds, and it was not until 1661 that a determined Dutchman named Arendt Van Curler ventured beyond Albany and established a new trading post. It was at a spot along the Mohawk River that the Indians called Schenectady—"the place beyond the open pines."

Van Curler's settlement grew into a village of some eighty houses enclosed by a wooden stockade. The settlers had little difficulty with the Mohawks until one February night in 1690 when a party of braves swooped down on the little village, killing sixty-nine people and burning seventy-eight of its houses. The attack, as the survivors discovered, was provoked by French forces from Canada who hoped to prevent other European settlers from making inroads on their own territory in the New World.

When the settlement at Schenectady was rebuilt in 1705, the English flag was hoisted over the new stockade. New York was now a British colony, but the next wave of settlers to move into the Iroquois country were not Englishmen but Germans, refugees from the Palatinate, a small nation along the Rhine, who had been driven from their homeland by the armies of France.

The Palatines originally fled to England. From there, they sailed to the colonies where they had been given a tract of land along the Mohawk River. Since they were supposed to provide protection against French attacks, they built their farmhouses to double as blockhouses. One of them, Fort Frey, still stands along Route 5 in the village of Palatine Bridge. Two others—Fort Wagner and Fort Klock—are not far away. The most historic fort along the old road, however, is Fort Johnson, a square stone house that was built in 1749 for Sir William Johnson, England's Superintendent of Indian Affairs.

Johnson arrived in the Mohawk Valley in 1738. A bold young Irishman, he had come to the New World to manage the extensive lands owned by his uncle, Sir Peter Warren. Johnson learned the Indians' language and customs, but he impressed them even more with his honesty. It was a rare white man who did not try to cheat an Indian in a bargain. Sir William's friendship with the Iroquois was cemented when he married an Indian girl, Molly Brant, who came to be known as "the brown Lady Johnson."

Joseph Brant, war chief of the Mohawks and adopted son of Sir William Johnson. (The Bettmann Archive)

He educated Molly's younger brother Joseph, and the two men remained friends after Joseph became a highly respected Mohawk Chief.

Sir William lived at Fort Johnson for ten years before moving to Johnson Hall in the present city of Johnstown. Both houses served as meeting places for the Indian leaders in the area. Sometimes as many as a thousand Iroquois would be camped around Fort Johnson for a powwow with "Warraghiyagey," or "Chief Big Business," as the Indians called their pale-faced friend.

It was almost entirely through Sir William Johnson's influence that the Iroquois fought on the side of the British in the French and Indian War. Very little of the fighting took place in this part of New York State, but it was a different story during the American Revolution. Sir William Johnson had died in 1774 but his son John remained loyal to the King. He and the Indian chief Joseph Brant and a Tory leader named Walter Butler led a series of vicious attacks against the American colonists along New York's western frontier.

There is a story that in one of their raids against the town of St. Johnsville, the Indians began shooting flaming arrows at the roof of an old stone church that had been built by Palatine settlers. Among the families who had helped erect it were the Nellises from nearby Nelliston. As the war party began their attack, one member of the family, a lieutenant with Butler's raiders, ordered the Indians to stop, and the church was saved.

At least one Dutch settler, Douw Fonda, refused to flee before the Tories and their Indian allies. During a raid in 1780, Fonda lost his life to a tomahawk and his home to a torch. His name survives as one of the cities along Route 5—Fonda, now the county seat of Montgomery County.

A better known hero of the American Revolution, General Nicholas Herkimer, also shares his name with a city. It was from Herkimer, then only a small fort, that the staunch son of Palatine immigrants marched out to meet the red-coated army of General Barry St. Leger.

St. Leger planned to cut across New York State from Lake Ontario while General Burgoyne marched down from Canada and General Howe north from New York. The three armies would then converge on Albany, use New York to cut New England off from the rest of the colonies and thus force the Americans to surrender.

St. Leger's forces, bolstered by a band of Indians led by Joseph Brant, hoped to begin their conquest of New York with an attack on Fort Stanwix (now the city of Rome). Calling out the 800 men of the county militia, Nicholas Herkimer prepared to march to the fort's defense. Before he could reach it, however, his army was ambushed by Indians in a ravine near Oriskany. The ensuing battle was one of the bloodiest of the Revolution.

Herkimer's horse was shot out from under him; the same cannon ball shattered the general's left leg. Undaunted, he ordered his men to carry his saddle to the foot of a near-by tree where he calmly lit his pipe and continued to direct the battle. The Americans suffered too many casualties to claim a victory, but they did succeed in forcing St. Leger's army to retreat without attacking Fort Stanwix, and the British plan for capturing New York was eventually abandoned.

After the battle, Nicholas Herkimer's leg had to be amputated and he died a few days later. His home and burial place are on the south side of the Mohawk River along Route 58, but his statue stands in Myers Park in the town of Herkimer on Route 5. His name on the pedestal is inscribed the way he wrote it, "Hercheimer."

The British surrender at Yorktown finally brought peace to the Mohawk Valley. Joseph Brant and his Iroquois warriors moved to Canada, and their lands were taken over by the government of the United States and given to soldiers who had fought in the Revolution. In many places, the forts that had been built for protection against Tory raids became the nuclei of new cities.

A German settlement that had been completely destroyed in 1776 was rebuilt and when it was incorporated as a city in 1798, the residents held a meeting at Baggs' Tavern to select a name. Utica was the one that was pulled out of the hat. A few years later, a former Dutch trading post near the site of the Iroquois' Great Council Fire on Onondaga Lake became the city of Syracuse. Its principal products were wooden plows and salt which came from some springs along the lake.

It seems a bit odd to find such ancient names as Utica and Syracuse in upper New York State, but the discovery of the buried Roman city of Pompeii in 1748 had inspired great popular enthusiasm for classical history and architecture. One result of this classical revival was that many American cities founded during the late 18th and early 19th centuries were given names like Athens, Troy and Rome.

As the population of western New York grew, the old Iroquois Trail quickly developed into a well traveled road. By 1797 traffic was so heavy that a turnpike was built between Albany and Schenectady. A few years later a second turnpike, the Mohawk, was established from Schenectady to Utica and a bridge was built across the Mohawk River to connect the two roads. A third turnpike was subsequently added between Utica and Buffalo. Early emigrants to the west had called this part of the trail the Great Genesee Road and it is still called Genesee Street in Syracuse and Utica. When it was incorporated as a turnpike, however, its legal name became the Seneca Road. Today all three turnpikes form the major part of New York State Highway 5.

The new turnpikes were not the only signs that upper New York State was becoming more civilized. In 1795, Union College was chartered in Schenectady. It was founded because the farmers in the region were reluctant to have their sons travel all the way to Harvard or Yale for a college education. Union was one of the first nonsectarian colleges in the United States. Later, it became the first to add science and modern languages to the curriculum, the first to have a planned campus and the first to organize school fraternities.

In 1793, Robert Morris, the man who had largely financed the

American Revolution, sold some three million acres of land in western New York to a group of Dutch investors. They in turn organized the Holland Land Company to resell the property in smaller lots to individual buyers. The company set up an office in Batavia, New York, and a man named Joseph Ellicott became their agent.

The Holland Land Company was responsible for the settlement of most of the countryside between the Genesee River and the Great Lakes. In fact, business was so brisk that the Batavia office is supposed to have inspired the phrase, "doing a land office business." The building still stands on West Main Street in Batavia and is now open to the public as a museum of western New York history.

Joseph Ellicott can also take credit for developing the city of Buffalo, New York. He first went there to map the site in 1799 and discovered little more than the remains of a French fort that had been destroyed by the British during the French and Indian War. Earlier, the spot had been visited by Robert La Salle, one of the early explorers of the Great Lakes. Ellicott began offering lots for sale in Buffalo in 1803. His brother Andrew, an army engineer who had helped lay out Washington, D.C., planned the new city and made Niagara Square its center.

One of the most accurate records we have of the early days of New York's Route 5 is in the journal kept by a Boston lawyer named Timothy Bigelow. In 1805 Bigelow and some friends embarked on a trip across New York State to Niagara Falls. They stopped at Schenectady, which Bigelow found "not to be a word fitted to common organs of speech. We heard it pronounced Snacktady, Snackedy, Ksnackidy, Ksnactady, Snackendy, and Snackady, which last is much the more common."

Another stop on the journey was at a tavern called Abel's on Trapp's Hill in Amsterdam. Bigelow liked the view—"an agreeable mixture of hills and plaines, diversified with extensive forests almost in a state of nature, and cultivated fields scarce less extensive now covered with a rich harvest of ripening wheat"—but he was less enthusiastic about the tavern itself. He called it "a poor one, and our dinner, of course, was miserable." He was far happier in Utica, where he found "good fare" and "in particular, good wine."

Farther along the road, the travelers passed through an Oneida Indian village and stopped to visit with an old Chief named Skenandoa. Although Bigelow doesn't mention it in his journal, Skenandoa was a great friend of the Reverend Samuel Kirkland, the Congregational minister who founded Hamilton College. Before the chief died in 1816 at the age of 110, he asked to be buried beside Samuel Kirkland so he could "climb into Heaven holding onto the Dominie's coattails."

Near Syracuse, Timothy Bigelow noted the site of the "Celebrated Onandaga salt springs" and in Canandaigua he met an old friend from Massachusetts who had just returned from "New Connecticut beyond Lake Erie." The reference is undoubtedly to the parcel of 500,000 acres in Huron and Erie Counties, Ohio, which the state of Connecticut had given to citizens whose homes had been burned in British attacks during the American Revolution.

Tourists like Timothy Bigelow and emigrants like those who settled "New Connecticut" used the Mohawk Turnpike and the Genesee Road, but in general traffic along the roads slowed with the opening of the Erie Canal in 1825. The canal provided a direct water route from Buffalo to Albany. From there boats could sail down the Hudson to New York.

During the next twenty-five years, railroads usurped most of the canal's freight and passenger business. Both types of transportation also contributed to the decline of Route 5, but at the same time they were responsible for the growth and development of the cities along its route. Today these cities are served by many roads, including New York State's major artery, the Governor Thomas E. Dewey Thruway.

Diminished in importance as a highway, the former Iroquois Trail is still interesting because it passes through so many places that have associations with America's history. Seneca Falls, for example, was the site of the first women's rights conference. It was called by Mrs. Elizabeth Cady Stanton in the summer of 1848, and among the women who attended were two other well-known feminists—Lucretia Mott and Amelia Jenks Bloomer.

Mrs. Stanton presented the assembled delegates with a Declaration of Principles that pointed out the need for better education for women and the right to hold jobs. When she also suggested that women be given the right to vote, her audience gasped in disbelief. Even the doughty Quakeress Lucretia Mott thought her old friend had gone too far. "Why Lizzie," she exclaimed, "thee will make us look ridiculous!"

Most of the early feminists were also dedicated abolitionists. In the years before the Civil War, Skaneateles, Syracuse and Auburn were stops on the Underground Railroad that smuggled fugitive slaves out of the south and helped them to freedom in Canada. Harriet Tubman, an ex-slave who was one of the most active workers for the cause, lived just outside of Auburn.

Another resident of that city, and another outspoken foe of slavery was William Seward. Seward, a graduate of Union College, practiced law in Auburn and occasionally handled legal work for the Holland Land Company. Active in Republican politics, he was elected governor of New York in 1838. In 1865, as Abraham Lincoln's Secretary of State, Seward was marked for assassination by the same band of conspirators who succeeded in murdering Lincoln. Although he, too, was attacked on the grim night of April 14th, the Secretary survived and lived to serve in President Andrew Johnson's cabinet. As Johnson's Secretary of State Seward was responsible for the purchase of Alaska from Russia. Seward retired to his home in Auburn in 1869 and died there three years later. His house still stands on South Street, and his grave is in Fort Hill Cemetery.

Another of Lincoln's appointees, General Francis W. E. Spinner, served as Treasurer of the United States from 1861 to 1875. Spinner, who came from Herkimer, was the first man to hire young women to work in federal offices. His statue, erected by a group of grateful "government girls," stands in Herkimer's Myers Park.

Two Presidents, Millard Fillmore and Grover Cleveland, lived in Buffalo and a third, William McKinley, died there. McKinley was shot by an anarchist while attending the Pan American Exposition in September 1901.

The decades just before and just after McKinley's administration were a period of tremendous industrial expansion. During this time, many of the cities along Route 5 grew into major manufacturing centers. Most of them have remained so to this day. Amsterdam is famous for carpets and Utica for sheets. Schenectady is the headquarters of the giant General Electric Company, which grew out of a machine works started by Thomas A. Edison in 1886.

The route west of Albany passes both farms and factories as it wends its way to Buffalo and then disappears into northern Pennsylvania. But there are still a few traces of the red men who first traveled on it. Utica boasts the Sacred Stone of the Oneida Indians, a massive ceremonial rock on which all their rituals were held. Excavations near Fonda have revealed the outlines of a dozen lodges and a stockade. The site was once the village of Caughnawaga, an Indian settlement from about 1667 to 1693. For ten of these years it was a French Jesuit mission and it was here that Kateri Tekakwitha, known as the Lily of the Mohawks, was converted to Christianity. Kateri, who died at the age of 19, was canonized as the first American saint.

At Waterloo the huge Patriarch Elm, some twenty feet in circumference, has been standing for over three hundred years, and on a hillside near Palatine Bridge a pair of craggy profiles called The Noses have been brooding over the countryside even longer. They probably know more than any historian about the state highway that passes beside them but they are doomed to stony silence.

5

U.S. 90 Trail of the Conquistadores

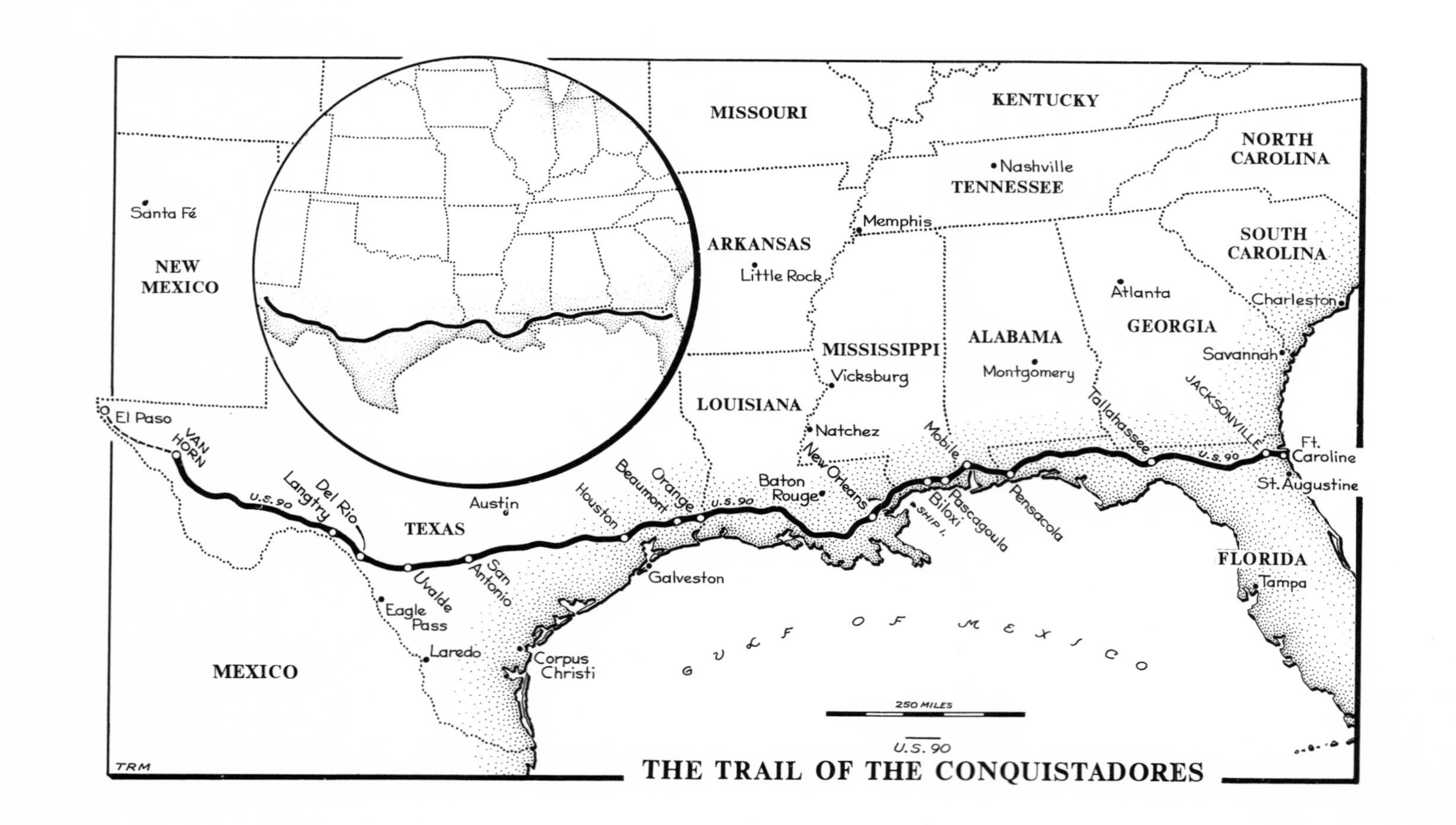

THE TRAIL OF THE CONQUISTADORES

U.S. 90 cuts across northern Florida from Jacksonville Beach to Pensacola. From there it follows the shores of the Gulf of Mexico through Alabama, Mississippi and Louisiana, veers off into Texas and ends abruptly about fifty miles from the Mexican border. The road passes through five states that have belonged at various times to seven different nations—Spain, France, England, Mexico, the Republic of Texas, the Confederacy and the United States.

The Spaniards were the first to arrive on the Gulf Coast. In the Spring of 1513 Juan Ponce de Leon landed on the shores of what he thought was an enormous island. Because it was the Easter Season, *Pascua Florida* in Spanish, Ponce de Leon named the island Florida. He hoped to start a colony there but when he returned a few years later he and his men were attacked by Indians and Ponce de Leon was killed.

Of the many other conquistadores, or conquerors, who tried to explore Florida, the most successful was Hernando De Soto, the discoverer of the great Mississippi River. Blazing a trail that may well have followed sections of the present Route 90, De Soto made his way across Florida, camped on the site of Mobile, Alabama, and marched as far west as Texas. The strong-willed conquistador died in the course of his expedition and his men buried him in the river he had discovered; then they built boats and sailed back to the Spanish outposts in Mexico.

De Soto and the other conquistadores claimed all the land along the Gulf of Mexico in the name of the King of Spain, but their claim was soon threatened by another European power. In

1564, a group of Huguenots—French Protestants who had been banished from their homeland—built a small fort near the present city of Jacksonville. The following year, the Spaniards built a fort of their own in Florida and sent an army to drive the French settlers from Fort Caroline. The Spanish fort grew into St. Augustine, the first permanent settlement in the United States. Fort Caroline was destroyed, but a replica of the outpost has been built only a few miles from Route 90, and is now a national memorial.

More than a hundred years passed before either France or Spain attempted any more settlements in the New World. Then in 1682, the French explorer La Salle rediscovered the Mississippi River. He took possession of the lands around it and named them Louisiana in honor of King Louis XIV of France.

La Salle returned to France to inform the King of the newest addition to his empire, but when he sailed back across the Atlantic to start a French settlement in Louisiana, his ships got lost and landed on the coast of Texas instead. La Salle was murdered by one of his followers before he could find his way back to the Mississippi, and Louisiana remained a no man's land for the next sixteen years.

In 1698 the Le Moyne brothers, the Sieur d'Iberville and the Sieur de Bienville, received a patent from King Louis XIV to establish a colony at the mouth of the Mississippi. They arrived with four ships and about 200 settlers. Between them the two brothers founded three of the most important cities along Route 90—Biloxi, Mississippi; Mobile, Alabama; and New Orleans, Louisiana.

When Spain decided to build up her defenses against the French intruders, two more cities were born. A fort was erected at Pensacola to protect Florida, and a half dozen missions, including San Antonio, were established in Texas.

The French and Indian War marked the first step in the decline of Europe's power in the New World. The treaty of Paris, which ended the war in 1763, forced France off the North American continent. England and Spain then divided her territory, England taking all the land east of the Mississippi and Spain all the land west of the river.

The map of North America changed again after the American Revolution. France regained the Louisiana Territory and England returned Florida to Spain. But this new division of land was equally short-lived. The Louisiana Purchase in 1803 signaled the departure of the French and in 1818, an American army led by General Andrew Jackson marched into Florida to keep peace between the Seminole Indians and the American and English settlers there. A year later Spain renounced her claim to Ponce de Leon's "island" and Florida was ceded to the United States.

Spain's power in North America finally ended with Mexico's revolt in 1821. Texas became a Mexican possession, the last of the Gulf Coast states to remain in the hands of a foreign power. The Texans solved the problem in 1836 with a revolt of their own. They established themselves as an independent nation and nine years later were annexed to the United States.

The sixth of the seven flags to fly over the Gulf Coast was the Stars and Bars of the Confederacy. It was replaced in 1865 by the Stars and Stripes. Today the lands that France and Spain once fought over are part of the United States, but memories of those earlier years are still very much alive along Route 90.

The road starts in the resort city of Jacksonville Beach, named, like Jacksonville, a few miles to the west, for Andrew Jackson, who served for a while as Florida's territorial governor. Jacksonville itself, one of Florida's largest cities, was once a cattle crossing on the St. John's River that the English called Cowford.

Jacksonville has been attacked in two wars: the Seminole War —which erupted between 1832 and 1843 when the United States tried to remove the Florida Indians from their lands—and the Civil War. During the War between the States, federal troops occupied the city four different times. When they finally left in 1863 most of it was in ruins. It has since been rebuilt and is now a thriving industrial and port city.

Tallahassee, Florida's capital, is the next major city along Route 90. The site was visited by De Soto during the winter of 1539–40. He and his men are said to have celebrated the first Christmas observed in the United States. Florida's capitol building, completed in 1845, stands at the summit of Tallahassee's highest hill, but when the state's first legislature convened in 1824, they had to meet in log cabins.

During its days as a British possession, Florida was divided into two territories, East Florida and West Florida. Pensacola, the one-time Spanish fort, was the principal city in the west. Today it is best known as the headquarters and training center of the United States Naval Air Force, but the remains of the Spanish fortifications, Fort Barrancas and Fort San Carlos, are still standing.

Seville Square at East Government and South Alcaniz Streets has the atmosphere of both England and Spain. The square is a pleasant park surrounded by elegant 19th century homes. On one side is the Pensacola Historic Museum. It is housed in Old Christ Church, a Union barracks during the Civil War and the oldest church building still standing in Florida.

Mobile, the first permanent white settlement in Alabama, was founded in 1710 by Jean Baptiste Le Moyne, the Sieur de Bienville. Although the city has its own Mardi Gras, almost as festive as the one in New Orleans, its old mansions and beautiful gardens are more Southern than French. One lovely house, Oakleigh, is furnished as it was in the years before the Civil War and is now a museum of local history.

As Alabama's only seaport, Mobile is famous for shipbuilding. The Confederate submarine *Hunley* was built here. The ship, hand-operated by its crew of nine, became the first submarine to sink an enemy vessel. On a February night in 1864, she drove a torpedo into the Union ship *Housatonic* anchored in Charleston Harbor, South Carolina. Unfortunately, the *Hunley* followed her victim to the bottom of the harbor.

Admiral Raphael Semmes, the Confederate naval hero, lived in

Mobile. Semmes was the commander of the notorious privateer *Alabama*. Launched in Liverpool, and armed in the Azores Islands, the *Alabama* became a major threat to the Union fleet. Before she was finally destroyed in 1864, the *Alabama* had sunk at least fifty ships and burned or captured many more. Another, later model ship of the same name has been preserved in Mobile. At USS *Alabama* Battleship Memorial Park, the World War II vessel *Alabama* serves as a memorial to the state's war heroes.

One of the most spectacular sights in the South is Bellingrath Gardens, twenty miles south of Mobile on U.S. 90. The gardens are the creation of Walter Duncan Bellingrath, the son of a German immigrant. Bellingrath made a fortune when, in 1903, he secured the exclusive rights to sell a new soft drink called Coca-Cola.

An avid fisherman, he took his former fishing camp, an 800-acre site along the Isle-Aux-Oises River, and transformed it into a showplace. One section of Bellingrath Gardens is natural woodland, but the rest is planted with dogwood, mountain laurel, camellias, roses and some 200 varieties of azaleas.

Mississippi, adjacent to Alabama, has about a hundred miles of frontage on the Gulf Coast. U.S. 90 runs parallel to the shoreline, passing through an area that is partly resort hotels and beaches, partly fishing wharves and shrimp canneries. Pascagoula, the first city along the route, has an Old Spanish Fort only a few blocks from Route 90. Built by the French but later surrendered to the Spaniards, the fort dates back to 1719. Its walls, over a foot thick, are huge pine timbers held together with primitive cement made from mud mixed with moss and oyster shells.

Pascagoula is famous for its "Singing River," which emits a strange music that sounds like a swarm of bees. The river sings loudest at twilight on warm summer evenings. Scientists have tried to explain the sound in several different ways—natural gas escaping from the river bed, sand scraping along the slate bottom, an underwater cave pulling against the current—but the residents of Pascagoula have a better story.

According to the legend, a young brave of the Pascagoula tribe fell in love with a Biloxi princess. The princess was already promised to another warrior and when her father, the Biloxi chief, discovered that she returned the young Indian's love, he summoned his braves to attack the Pascagoulas. The Biloxi war party was so large that the Pascagoulas, knowing they were doomed, joined hands and walked into the river singing.

Biloxi, Mississippi, was the first permanent settlement in the Mississippi River Valley. It began at Ocean Springs, a few miles east of the city, where a fort was built by the Sieur d'Iberville in 1699. The entire Gulf Coast from Biloxi to New Orleans was severely damaged by Hurricane Camille in 1969. Many homes were destroyed in the storm, but two of Biloxi's best known landmarks escaped. One, the Biloxi Lighthouse, dates back to 1848. It was operated for half a century by two women, a mother and her daughter. When Abraham Lincoln was assassinated in 1865, Biloxi's citizens painted the 65-foot tower black.

Biloxi's other famous landmark, Beauvoir, is five miles west of the town on U.S. 90. Beauvoir is the house in which Jefferson Davis, president of the Confederate States of America, spent his final years. Davis bought the house in 1877 and lived there until his death in 1889. He spent part of those twelve years working on his book, *The Rise and Fall of the Confederate Government.* Visitors can stroll through the house and the adjacent museum and see Davis' desk and books in the Library Cottage where he worked.

By the beginning of the 18th century, the French had founded several settlements in the Mississippi River Valley, but they knew that families were needed to turn a settlement into a permanent colony. In 1721, eighty girls selected by a French bishop were imported as wives for the men in Mississippi. The first contingent of girls landed near Gulfport. They were called "filles à la cassette" because they carried their belongings in chests or "cassettes."

Six miles offshore from Gulfport on Ship Island is old Fort Massachusetts. A federal fortress when the Civil War began, the fort was later taken over by Confederates, then recaptured by Union forces and used to house Southern prisoners of war.

The town of Pass Christian, another stop on Route 90, received its unusual name from Christian L'Adnier. L'Adnier, one of the Sieur d'Iberville's crewmen, sailed into the bay thinking he had discovered a deep water pass from the Gulf of Mexico to Louisiana's Lake Pontchartrain.

Pass Christian gave its name to a naval battle that was actually fought a few miles away in Bay St. Louis. In 1814 five American gunboats tried to delay a fleet of sixty British ships sailing to the defense of New Orleans. All five of the American ships were sunk, but the British forces were defeated anyway. The engagement was the last naval battle fought against a foreign power in American waters.

The first city Route 90 enters in Louisiana is New Orleans. It was founded in 1718 by Jean Baptiste Le Moyne, the Sieur de Bienville and named for the Duke of Orleans.

The most historic section of New Orleans is the Vieux Carré or "old square." Among the buildings here is the Cabildo, where the administrators of Louisiana had their headquarters during the years when it was a Spanish possession. The signing of the Louisiana Purchase Agreement took place at the Cabildo in 1803. At Jackson Square, also in the Vieux Carré, the United States flag was raised over the new territory for the first time.

Among the other points of interest in New Orleans are St. Louis Cathedral, which dates back to 1794, and the Pontalba Apartments, which were built in 1849 and were the first apartment houses in the United States.

Although the flavor of New Orleans is predominantly French, only two buildings survive from its early days as a French colony. One is the Ursuline Convent begun in 1727, which now serves as the rectory for St. Mary's Catholic Church. The other, Madame John's Legacy, is a private home.

Chalmette National Historical Park, six miles north of New Orleans, was the scene of one of the most dramatic battles of the War of 1812. In January 1815, the British General, Sir Edward Pakenham, attacked New Orleans and was defeated by General Andrew Jackson. Unknown to both sides, the war had ended two weeks before. The battle, although not a decisive one, made Andrew Jackson famous and launched him on the road to the Presidency.

From New Orleans west to the Texas State line, U.S. 90 bisects a region of bayous and moss-draped cypress trees that is known as Acadiana or Cajunland. The French-speaking Cajuns are the descendants of an earlier group of Frenchmen who once lived in Nova Scotia. They founded the Canadian colony of Acadia and lived there for over 150 years until the English drove them out in 1755. Four thousand Acadians were exiled from their homeland. Some of them found refuge in Maryland and Virginia; others in the West Indies. Many more came to Louisiana.

The story of Acadia has been immortalized in Henry Wadsworth Longfellow's poem, "Evangeline." It tells of a pair of young lovers, Evangeline and Gabriel, who became separated in the exodus from Acadia. They met again many years later when Gabriel was dying in a Philadelphia hospital and the snowy-haired Evangeline became his nurse.

St. Martinsville, less than ten miles from U.S. 90, is the place where the Evangeline story is best remembered. Longfellow-Evangeline Memorial Park has a museum housed in the building that was once the home of Louis Arceneaux, said to be the original Gabriel of Longfellow's tale. The Cajuns have another version of the story. After being separated from Evangeline, Arceneaux is supposed to have married another. Eventually Evangeline found her way to St. Martinsville and when she discovered what had happened, died of a broken heart.

The grave of Emmeline Labiche, who is thought to be the real-life Evangeline, is in the cemetery of St. Martin of Tours Church.

The grave of the "real-life" Evangeline.

It is marked by a statue of the French maiden donated and posed for by the actress Dolores Del Rio, who once played the role of Evangeline in the movies.

U.S. 90's first stop in Texas is Orange, a favorite meeting place of Jean Lafitte's pirates. Lafitte operated out of Galveston, but he and his men were apt to appear in almost any of the ports along the Gulf coast. At Lafitte's insistence a large band of his followers assisted Andrew Jackson in the defense of New Orleans.

Beaumont, not far from Orange, is noted for another kind of treasure. On January 10, 1901, a gush of slimy black liquid spouted out of the Spindletop oil well and shot 200 feet in the air. The discovery launched the oil boom that created so many Texas millionaires.

Houston, the Lone Star State's largest city, is also on U.S. 90. The city was founded in 1836, the same year that Texas won her independence from Mexico. Houston is so big, busy and modern, it seems hard to believe that a steamboat captain once sailed up Buffalo Bayou—now part of the Houston Ship Canal—without even noticing that there was a city on the shore. He had to back up to land.

A few miles outside of Houston is San Jacinto Battleground, where the city's namesake scored his greatest victory. On April 21, 1836, Sam Houston attacked the Mexican general Santa Anna at San Jacinto, defeated his army and took Santa Anna prisoner. The battle ended the war against Mexico and established Texas as an independent republic.

A more famous landmark in the Texans' struggle against Mexico is the Alamo in San Antonio. The old mission of San Antonio de Valerio, better known as the Alamo, was under siege by Santa Anna's forces from February 23rd to March 6, 1836. All 187 of the men who tried to defend it were killed, including Jim Bowie, Davy Crockett and the commander of the makeshift fortress, Colonel William B. Travis. "Remember the Alamo!" became the rallying cry at San Jacinto, where the Mexicans were finally defeated.

The Alamo. (Courtesy San Antonio Chamber of Commerce)

San Antonio is a startling combination of colonial Spain and contemporary America. The Alamo stands amidst glassy hotels and office buildings. Not far away is the Spanish Governor's Palace, which was built around 1749, and the San Fernando Cathedral, which dates back to 1738.

There are several old Spanish missions within an easy drive from San Antonio. One of the most picturesque is Mission San Jose at San Jose Mission State and National Historic Park. The brown sandstone church with its delicately carved rose window is one of the most photographed buildings in the United States.

After leaving San Antonio, U.S. 90 heads west toward the Rio Grande River, the boundary between Mexico and the United States. Along the way, it passes through Uvalde, the home of John Nance Garner. Garner was Speaker of the House of Representatives and also served two terms as Vice President of the United States under President Franklin Delano Roosevelt. His house, now a museum, has an interesting exhibit of the gavels he collected during his years as presiding officer of the House of Representatives and the Senate.

The Judge Roy Bean Museum is on Route 90 in the tiny town of Langtry on the Rio Grande. Judge Bean proclaimed himself "the only law west of the Pecos" and, like many justices of the peace in the old West, performed his duties with a single law book and a six-shooter. Langtry was originally named Vinegaroon, but the name was changed on the Judge's orders because Lily Langtry was his favorite actress. He also named the saloon next to his court the Jersey Lily in her honor. There is a replica of the old saloon in the Whitehead Memorial Museum in Del Rio, 59 miles away.

U.S. 90 ends over 1500 miles from where it began, in the sheep- and cattle-raising town of Van Horn. To some travelers, it may seem like an ordinary road, but those who have read its story know better. Like so many of America's highways, it reflects hundreds of years of history in a single ribbon of concrete.

6

The Natchez Trace Parkway

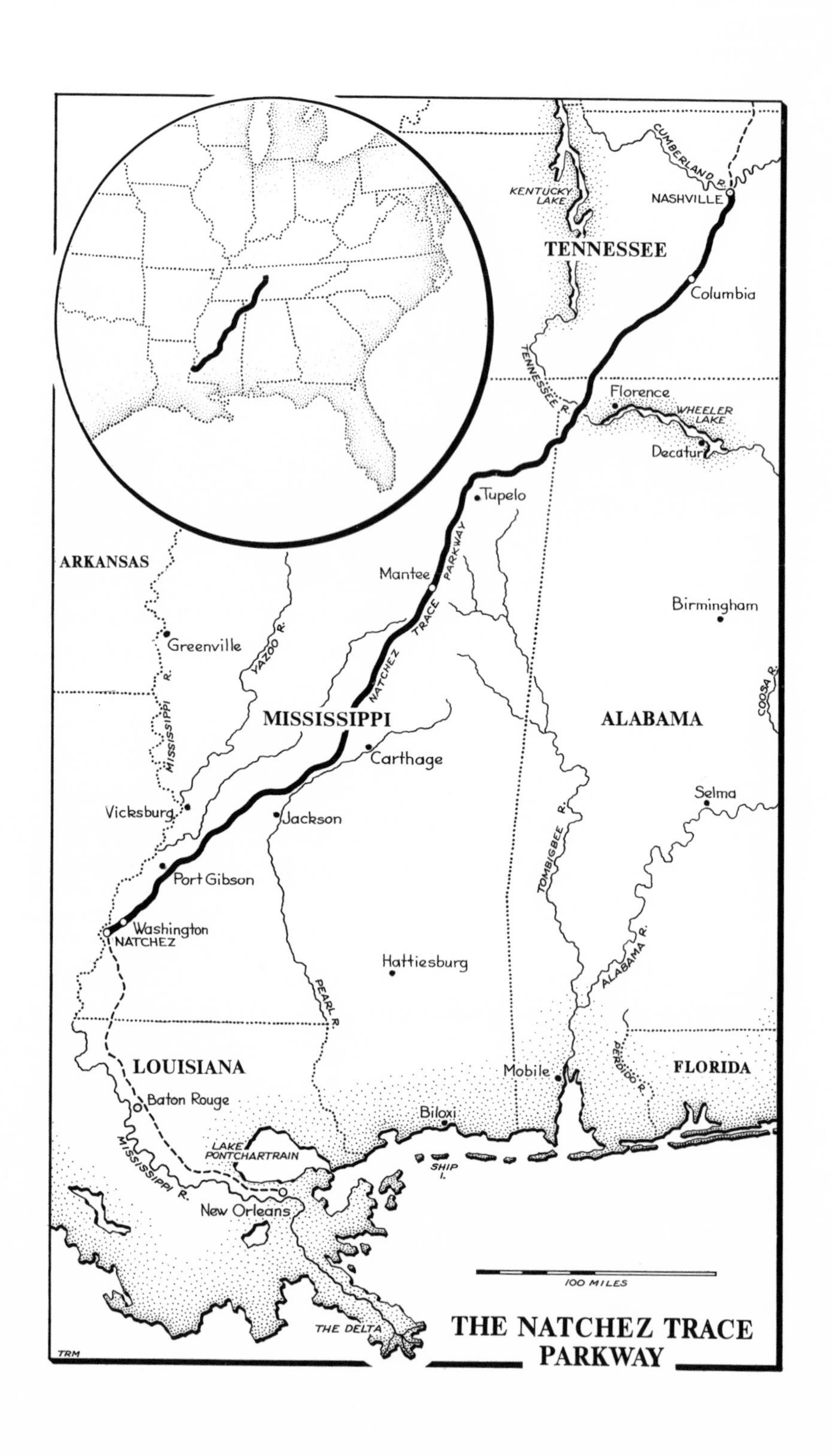
KENTUCKY LAKE
CUMBERLAND R.
NASHVILLE
TENNESSEE
Columbia
TENNESSEE R.
Florence
WHEELER LAKE
Decatur
Tupelo
ARKANSAS
Mantee
NATCHEZ TRACE PARKWAY
Birmingham
Greenville
YAZOO R.
MISSISSIPPI R.
COOSA R.
MISSISSIPPI
ALABAMA
Carthage
Selma
Vicksburg
Jackson
TOMBIGBEE R.
Port Gibson
Washington
NATCHEZ
ALABAMA R.
Hattiesburg
PEARL R.
PERDIDO R.
LOUISIANA
Mobile
FLORIDA
Baton Rouge
Biloxi
LAKE PONTCHARTRAIN
SHIP I.
MISSISSIPPI R.
New Orleans
100 MILES
THE DELTA
TRM
THE NATCHEZ TRACE PARKWAY

The Natchez Trace Parkway has been built along the path of the old Natchez Trace, for years the only road between Natchez, Mississippi, and Nashville, Tennessee. The route was called a trace—meaning a line of footprints—by the French who first settled Natchez in 1716. They found the path already marked out, worn first by buffalo making their way to the salt licks near the Mississippi River, and later by the Choctaw and Chickasaw Indians who lived in the forests it passed through.

French missionaries and traders used the Trace to travel into the Indians' territory, and later when Mississippi was acquired by England, the route became known as "The Path to the Choctaw Nation." The Spanish occupied Mississippi for a brief time after the American Revolution, but in 1795 the territory was ceded to the United States.

A few years later, Secretary of State Timothy Pickering complained about delays in the mail delivery to Mississippi. The letters traveled by ship and it took longer to get a message to Washington from Natchez, Pickering maintained, than it did to get one from Paris.

At Pickering's suggestion, the Natchez Trace was designated a post road and in 1800 the first post rider was dispatched from Nashville. On the day he was scheduled to arrive in Natchez, everyone in town turned out to greet him. The well-wishers crowded around the postmaster as he opened the historic mail bag, but instead of the letters and packets they had expected to see him pull from it, there was only a soggy lump of paper. Weeks of traveling through swamps and bayous had taken their toll of the United States Mail.

The following year the road was improved by troops working under orders from General James Wilkinson, commander of the United States Army in the west. Their efforts made the Trace a little more passable, but there was still no guarantee that the mail would arrive safely. The postmaster always gave the rider six weeks' leeway. If he failed to show up by then, it was announced that he was "presumed lost." Any number of disasters might have befallen him, from drowning in a bayou to being murdered by bandits.

Next to the post riders, the most frequent travelers along the Natchez Trace were residents of the Ohio River Valley. They were called "Kaintucks," whether they hailed from Ohio, Illinois or Kentucky.

The Appalachian Mountains were too steep for the Kaintucks to carry their produce across, so the pioneer farmers transported it down the Ohio River to the Mississippi on rafts and flatboats. They brought wheat and flour, barrels of pork, hides, tobacco and furs and sold them all in the busy port of Natchez.

The Kaintucks' broad flatboats were easy to row down river, but the tides and currents made it impossible to get them back upstream. It was better to sell them for timber and walk back home along the Natchez Trace.

To save money, the Kaintucks sometimes became ride-and-tie men. Two of them would chip in and buy a horse. One man rode all morning while the other walked. At noontime, the morning rider hitched the horse to a tree and started walking. When the first man reached the horse, it was his turn to ride. He kept going until he caught up with his partner. Then they camped for the night and resumed their journey in the morning.

One of the hundreds of flatboatmen who used the Natchez Trace was a Kentucky farmer named Thomas Lincoln, who took the road on his way home to marry Nancy Hanks in 1806.

Twenty-two years later, their long-legged son Abe also brought a cargo down the Mississippi on a flatboat, but he did not have to walk home as his father had. By then steamboats had conquered the Mississippi currents, and travelers could ride upstream as well as down.

During the heyday of the Trace, Natchez was divided into two distinctly different cities. The stately mansions of wealthy planters stood on the bluffs overlooking the river. Beneath them along the waterfront were the saloons and gambling houses of Natchez-under-the-hill. Here the Kaintucks often went looking for a few shots of whiskey and a peek at the dance hall girls. In the process, they might also be fleeced by professional gamblers or have their pockets picked by barroom toughs.

Stanton Hall, a Natchez mansion.

The flatboatmen who managed to get out of Natchez with the silver from the sale of their produce still jingling in their pockets had other dangers to face on their journey home.

The Natchez Trace was a notorious hideout for thieves and cutthroats. In some places, steep walls of earth, often as high as twenty-five feet, rose up on either side of the road. Combined with the thick foliage and moss-hung trees, they created gloomy passageways that invited trouble.

One of the most dreaded of the desperados who lurked along the Natchez Trace was John Murrell. Murrell's mother taught him to steal when he was only ten years old. After that he took anything he could lay his hands on—slaves, silver, or horses. When it was necessary to kill his victims, Murrell disposed of their bodies by stuffing them with stones and sinking them in the swamps.

Another notorious outlaw, Samuel Mason, liked to bury his victims along the Trace and mark their graves with a sign giving their names and the dates they were murdered. Sometimes he carved "Done by Mason of the Woods" on a nearby tree.

Mason worked with several accomplices, including another deadly outlaw, Little Harpe, and a supposedly respectable merchant named Anthony Glass. Glass regularly visited the taverns of Natchez-under-the-hill and tipped Mason off when a traveler with a particularly full moneybag was about to start on a trip along the Trace.

Mason was captured in 1803 in what was then Spanish territory on the far side of the Mississippi. The Spaniards tried him and his friend Little Harpe and each confessed to a long list of misdeeds that he swore the other was responsible for. Since most of their crimes had been committed on American soil, the Spanish officials shipped them back to Mississippi.

Mason and Little Harpe managed to escape when a storm came up and capsized the boat that was returning them to Natchez. But the two fugitives then began quarreling with each other. Little Harpe was infuriated because Mason had betrayed him at their trial. He sneaked up on him one night and killed him with a tomahawk. Harpe then cut off his old friend's head, rolled it in blue clay to keep it from putrefying and brought it to the courthouse in one of the towns along the Trace. There he presented the head and demanded the $2000 reward that Governor William Claiborne had offered for Mason's capture, dead or alive. Before he could collect the money, however, Harpe himself was recognized, recaptured and promptly hanged. His head was cut off and placed on a pole beside the Trace as a warning to other outlaws.

Thomas Jefferson's purchase of the Louisiana Territory in 1803 brought more traffic to the Natchez Trace as emigrants began heading into the still uncharted lands beyond the Mississippi. In 1806 Jefferson signed into law a bill stipulating that the trail was to be turned into a road "12 feet in width and passable for a wagon."

By a tragic coincidence, the road that Jefferson had done so much to establish became the death place of one of his most valued friends. Meriwether Lewis, the explorer of the Northwest Territory, began his career in government service as Jefferson's personal secretary. When Jefferson decided that the lands between the Mississippi and the Pacific Ocean should be charted, he appointed the youthful Lewis to lead an expedition across the continent.

Lewis selected William Clark as his companion and the two men set out in the winter of 1804. When they returned from the hazardous trip almost two years later, they were acclaimed as heroes. Soon after that Jefferson rewarded Lewis for his services to the nation by making him governor of Louisiana.

While on a trip back to Washington in 1809 the 35-year-old governor stopped for the night at an inn called Grinder's Stand. At daybreak Mrs. Grinder found him lying in his bed, a gunshot wound in his forehead. He died about two hours later.

Although some historians believe that Lewis was murdered, it seems more likely that he committed suicide. He was subject to

Meriwether Lewis. (Culver Pictures)

fits of depression, and his aides had been so concerned about his dark moods that two weeks earlier they had refused to let him have any gunpowder lest he try to take his own life.

Today Meriwether Lewis Park occupies the former site of Grinder's Stand. In 1848 the state of Tennessee erected a monument to the explorer. It is a broken stone shaft—a symbol of his life cut off in its prime. Carved at the base are the words that Thomas Jefferson used to commend the young hero on his return from the Northwest Territory: "His courage was undaunted. His firmness and perseverance yielded to nothing but impossibilities."

There were dozens of other inns or stands along the old Natchez Trace. One, the Mount Locust Stand, has been rebuilt by the National Park Service and looks exactly as it did in 1820. Travelers who stopped at the stands paid twelve and a half cents for their lodgings. For that sum, they not only had to put up with sleeping three in a bed, they also had to worry about waking up to find their money gone, or—an even worse fate—not waking up at all.

A few of the stand owners made a habit of murdering their guests and stealing their valuables. In Mississippi and Tennessee thieves were punished by having their ears cropped or their thumbs branded. Wise travelers always studied an innkeeper closely before deciding whether to stay with him for the night.

One enterprising Trace resident, George Colbert, did not have to resort to robbery to make his fortune on the road. Colbert, part Scotch and part Chickasaw Indian, had persuaded his fellow tribesmen to let the United States government build the road through their lands. In return, Colbert was given the right to operate the only ferry across the Tennessee River. He made the most of it, charging exorbitant fares and further bilking the travelers when they stopped for supplies at the trading post he owned near the ferry slip.

Andrew Jackson had many adventures along the Natchez Trace. For awhile he owned a trading post on Bayou Pierre and he often traveled back and forth to Nashville. He returned from one trip with a lively dark-eyed wife, a divorcee named Rachel Robards. Jackson and his bride lived for awhile in his log cabin near Port Gibson. Later he bought a tract of land thirteen miles east of Nashville and built the stately white columned Hermitage where he and his beloved Rachel are both buried.

In addition to the wedding journey he took with Rachel, Jackson made another memorable trip along the Natchez Trace. During the War of 1812, he was commissioned a Major General in the United States Army and sent from Tennessee with an army of 2000 volunteers to reinforce General James Wilkinson in New Orleans.

Jackson's cavalry rode down the Trace while his foot soldiers traveled by boat. They met at Natchez, set up camp in the town of Washington about four miles away and waited for General Wilkinson to summon them to New Orleans.

The orders never came from Wilkinson. Instead, after three weeks of waiting, Jackson received a letter from the Secretary of War in Washington informing him that his troops were no longer required. He was to dismiss them at once and send them home.

It was an incredible command. The men were 500 miles from Tennessee. 150 of them were sick. They were short of wagons and supplies and the army had provided no funds to buy any. Jackson advanced money from his own pocket for provisions. He and his officers gave up their horses so the men who were sick could ride. Then he set out to lead the bedraggled army back to Nashville.

The soldiers were impressed at the way their commanding officer took care of them and shared their hardships on the miserable journey. In tribute to his perseverance and courage, they gave him the nickname he was to keep for life—Old Hickory.

In 1814 Andrew Jackson again went to the defense of New Orleans and this time scored a spectacular victory against the British. He rode back along the Trace in style and was given a rousing welcome everywhere he stopped.

Some years before Jackson's experiences on the Trace, another well known, but less respected, figure in American history also traveled along the road.

After his duel with Alexander Hamilton in 1804, Aaron Burr

fled south to escape arrest. Duels were still legal in this part of the country and few southerners condemned Burr for Hamilton's death. Instead he was accorded all the hospitality that befitted his position as a former Senator from New York and former Vice President of the United States. Andrew Jackson gave a banquet for him in Nashville and General James Wilkinson sent a barge manned by ten of his strongest soldiers to transport him down river to New Orleans.

In the course of his travels, Burr also visited Natchez and returned to Nashville along the Natchez Trace. He described it in a letter to his daughter Theodosia as "four hundred and fifty miles of wilderness."

Burr may have made other trips along the Trace. By now he was involved in a scheme with General James Wilkinson and an eccentric Irishman named Harman Blennerhassett. The three of them planned to raise an army, take over a large chunk of American and Spanish territory in the southwest and create an empire with Burr as its head.

Burr had several conspiratorial meetings with Blennerhassett at Connelly's Tavern, which still stands in Natchez, but their plot was betrayed by Wilkinson. The General, undoubtedly expecting rewards from both countries, warned the President of the United States and the Viceroy of Mexico of the scheme.

Burr and Blennerhassett were arrested and brought to the town of Washington on the Natchez Trace for a hearing. It was held under a pair of enormous oak trees on the campus of Jefferson College. The judge who heard the case decided there was not enough evidence to put Burr on trial, but he asked him to reappear in court for a second hearing a few days later.

Instead of remaining in Natchez as the court had ordered him, Burr decided to flee. Disguised in tattered farmer's clothes, he started riding towards the Alabama line. He had not gotten far when he was recognized by a young lawyer, Nicholas Perkins, who noticed his shiny boots.

Burr was again arrested and he and Harman Blennerhasset were ordered to be tried on charges of treason and conspiracy in a court at Richmond, Virginia. Blennerhassett made the trip along the Natchez Trace complaining, in a letter to his wife, of "almost incessant perspiration" and "myriads of mosquitoes and horseflies."

Neither Burr nor his co-conspirator was found guilty, but Burr's reputation was further ruined by the trial. He left the United States and fled to England, while Blennerhassett retired to a plantation called LaCache in Port Gibson.

By the middle of the 1820's, steamboats had taken almost all of the traffic away from the Natchez Trace. Once over 20,000 travelers had made their way along the treacherous road each year. Now the trail was all but abandoned.

Local historical societies tried to keep both the Trace and its memories alive, but it was almost a hundred years before their efforts were rewarded. During the Great Depression of the 1930's President Franklin D. Roosevelt set up the Works Progress Administration to provide unemployed men with jobs building bridges, highways and public buildings.

At the instigation of some of his history-conscious constituents, Congressman Thomas Jefferson Busby of Mississippi suggested that one of the projects be launched in his home state. He asked the Department of the Interior to make "a survey of the old Indian trail known as the Natchez Trace . . . with a view to constructing a national road on this route to be known as the Natchez Trace Parkway."

The precise route of the original Trace is not really known, but the modern parkway comes as close to it as historians can judge and highway engineers consider practical.

Travelers on the Natchez Trace of the twentieth century can picnic in the woods where Sam Mason and Little Harpe once lurked or camp at a site where Andrew Jackson and his soldiers may have spent the night. Wherever they stop they are apt to find historical markers and monuments, and in some places they can actually walk along sections of the old Trace. The serene and scenic Natchez Trace Parkway is a highway steeped in history. Few roads have a prouder past.

7

U.S. 40 The Great National Turnpike

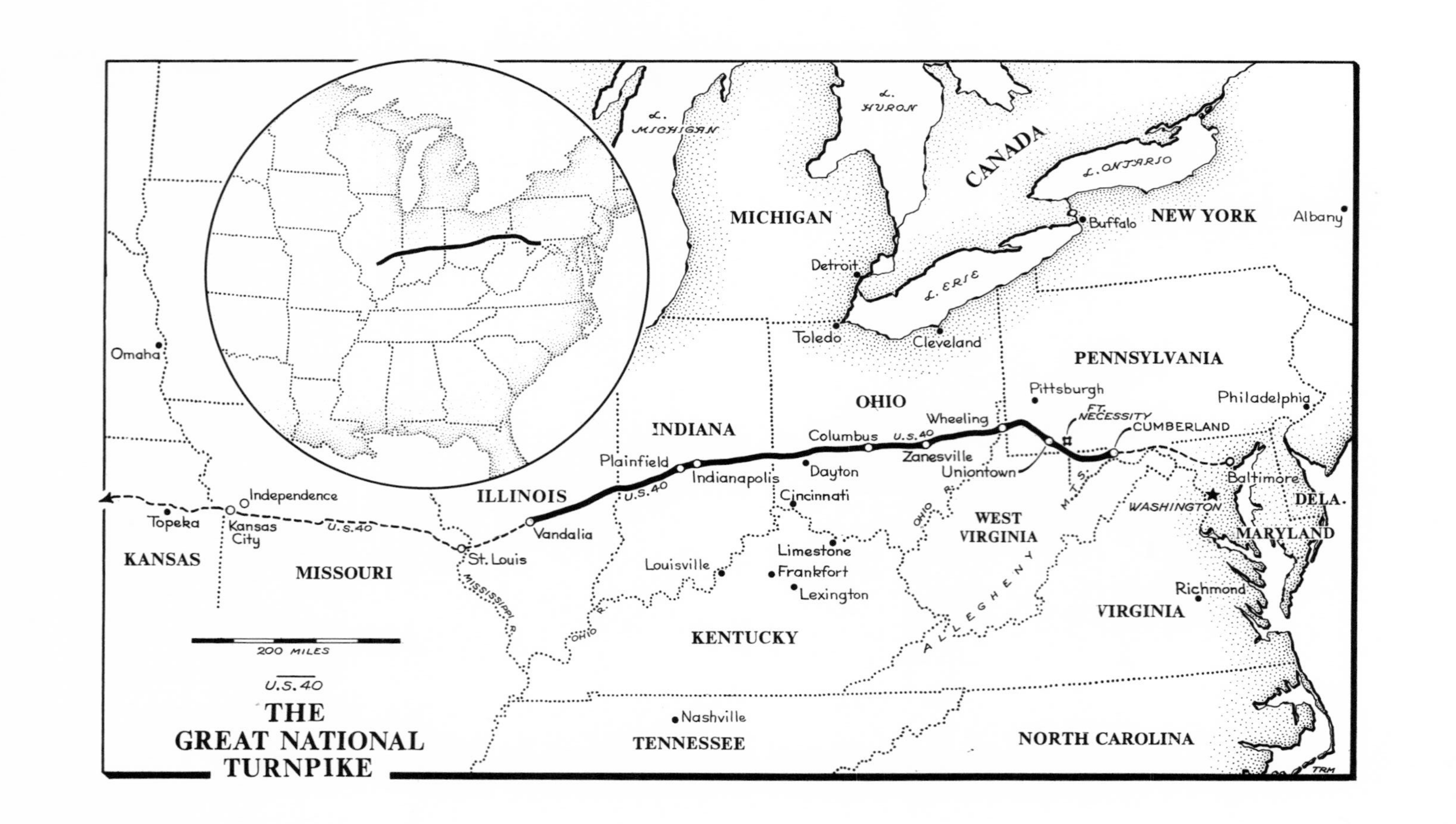

THE GREAT NATIONAL TURNPIKE

Like most of America's early roads, U.S. 40 began as a narrow path. The original trail was blazed by a Delaware Indian chief named Nemacolin. In 1749 he and a Maryland frontiersman, Thomas Cresap, marked out a sixty-mile path from a trading post near Will's Creek on the Potomac River in northwestern Maryland across the Allegheny Mountains to the Monongahela River in southwestern Pennsylvania.

Nemacolin's Path was used mainly by trappers and traders until, in 1753, it suddenly became a military road. In November of that year, a tall sandy-haired young major in the Virginia militia rode into the settlement at Will's Creek and asked for a guide to take him over the Alleghenies and into the wilderness beyond.

The officer was George Washington and he was on a special mission for the Royal Governor of Virginia. French troops had come down from Canada and were fortifying strategic points in Ohio and western Pennsylvania. Washington was on his way to warn the French that they were invading English territory.

Major Washington returned to Virginia some weeks later with the news that the French refused to abandon their forts. Soon after that he was again marching along Nemacolin's Path, this time at the head of a column of militia. The soldiers proceeded to the Great Meadows, near the Pennsylvania end of the path, and built a camp which they called Fort Necessity. The Virginians won a brief engagement against a small band of Indians and French-Canadians, but when a larger force returned for a reprisal raid, the militiamen were forced to retreat back over the mountains for safety.

The battle at Fort Necessity was the first skirmish of the French and Indian War. The war began in earnest when the British commander, General Edward Braddock, arrived in America a few months later with an army of 2000 men. Washington's troops had already built a fort at Will's Creek and named it Mt. Pleasant. When Braddock joined them there, he promptly rechristened the place Fort Cumberland in honor of the same man for whom the Cumberland Gap was named—King George II's son, the Duke of Cumberland.

Braddock planned to march head-on into the disputed territory and drive the French and their Indian allies out by force. But he could not do it unless Nemacolin's Path was made wide enough for a full scale army with a train of heavy artillery, baggage, medicine and supply wagons. Braddock ordered his engineers to clear a twelve-foot-wide road across the mountains.

Working sometimes with axes, sometimes with only their bare hands, the soldiers hacked their way through dense underbrush and trees that had been standing for centuries. It took six hundred engineers almost six weeks to clear a road long enough for the British army to begin their advance on the enemy.

It was a slow march—four miles of men and equipment inching their way through the forest like a giant scarlet serpent. Braddock's engineers had sunk paving blocks into the dirt to support the artillery, but in spite of their precautions, the heavy cannons frequently sank into the soft earth. Wagons were ruined on the rocky road, horses died from exhaustion, and more than one British infantryman collapsed in a ditch with stomach cramps and fever.

Unknown to General Braddock, his progress was carefully watched by Indian spies. When he reached the Great Meadows near the site of George Washington's defeat a year before, an enemy force suddenly swooped down in a surprise attack. Nine hundred of Braddock's men were killed; the rest retreated in disarray. The General himself was mortally wounded. His aides carried him to the ruins of Fort Necessity and when he died, buried him by the side of the road that for the next few years would bear his name.

Not many travelers ventured along Braddock's Road after the bloody battle on the Pennsylvania meadows. By the time the French and Indian War ended in 1763, however, most of the fighting had moved into upper New York State and Canada. A few hardy colonists decided to strike out for the country beyond the Alleghenies.

Among the pioneers was an enterprising Virginian named Ebenezer Zane. In 1759 Zane pushed twenty miles beyond Nemacolin's Path and Braddock's Road and established a trading post at a place on the Ohio River he called Wheeling.

As Zane had foreseen, a steady trickle of Americans was starting to move away from the Atlantic coastline. Some, heading for Kentucky, traveled along the Cumberland Road as far as Wheeling. They stopped at Ebenezer Zane's trading post and stocked up on salt pork, medicine and ammunition; then they traded their horses and wagons for passage on a flatboat down the Ohio River. It would have been easier and safer to make the journey to northern Kentucky by land, but the only road out of Wheeling was a footpath through the woods.

In 1796 Ebenezer Zane petitioned Congress for the rights to the land along the slender path. In exchange, he agreed to replace it with a road and to provide ferry service across all the rivers between Wheeling and the trail's end at Limestone, Kentucky.

The new road was called Zane's Trace. It continued in the westward direction of the old Cumberland Road for about sixty miles, then veered south into Kentucky. At the bend in the road, two of Ebenezer Zane's brothers, Silas and Jonathan, set up another trading post and immortalized the family name by calling the place Zanesville.

In the next few decades thousands of travelers set out on

Zane's Trace. Not all of them followed it to the end. Many took the road into Ohio and went no further. Others beat a still longer trail westward into the rich farmlands of Indiana and Illinois.

By 1800 it was obvious that America was going to be made up of many more states than the original thirteen that had won their independence from England. It was also obvious that a way must be found to keep the new states and the old united. At the urging of President Thomas Jefferson, Congress in 1806 voted to pave and grade the old wagon trail out of Cumberland and connect east and west with a Great National Turnpike.

It was a tremendous undertaking. A sixty-six-foot-wide thoroughfare had to be cleared, hills leveled, tree stumps dug out, roots, rock and surplus earth hauled away. The actual construction of the road did not begin until 1811 and it was over a year before the first ten miles were completed.

The work went a little faster after that and by 1818 a newspaper editor in Wheeling boasted that "the National Turnpike from Fort Cumberland to this place is in a considerable state of forwardness and promises fair to be one of the best and most permanent roads in the United States."

The supporters of the new highway had hoped that it would eventually be paved all the way to St. Louis, but it took six years to complete the section from Wheeling to Zanesville and five to get as far as Columbus. It was almost ten years before the turnpike went past Indiana and into Illinois and, as a Federal project, it was never completed beyond Vandalia. The state had to finish the last sixty miles to St. Louis.

For almost fifty years, the National Road was the busiest highway in the country. Freight wagons accounted for a large share of the traffic. From the east came clocks, glassware, nails and shoes; from the west, buffalo robes, tobacco, potatoes and corn.

The freight wagons were usually equipped with a set of brass bells strung on an iron arch and fastened to their harnesses. On mountain curves, the bells served to warn other drivers that someone was approaching from the opposite direction. If a teamster had the misfortune to get stuck in a ditch, it was the custom of the road to give the bells to the driver who pulled him out.

In addition to freight, livestock were a common sight along the turnpike. Drovers with herds of cattle, pigs or turkeys trudged along the road, driving the animals to the slaughterhouses in Baltimore or still farther away to Philadelphia or New York.

But the majority of travelers on the National Road were emigrants. In the heyday of the great turnpike, the population of Ohio, Indiana and Illinois increased from about 800,000 to well over 3 million. Some of the settlers were new Americans recently arrived from Ireland, Germany or Sweden; some were old Americans from New England, New Jersey or New York. They came on horseback or in carts but the most popular conveyance was the lumbering Conestoga wagon. It was large enough to hold a family and all their possessions, and its white canvas top provided ample protection from sun, wind and rain.

By 1830, the traffic also included stagecoaches that carried mail and passengers to all points along the National Road. The coaches bore such elegant names as *Ivanhoe, Natchez* or *Henry Clay,* but regular riders soon dubbed them "Shake-guts" or "Spankers" because of their effects on their passengers' anatomy.

The National Road was icy in winter, dusty in summer, muddy in spring and fall, but sooner or later almost everyone of importance in America had occasion to use it. In 1825 Lafayette traveled along the Pennsylvania section on his visit to the United States, and commented on the excellent service at the Walker House in Uniontown.

A more frequent visitor to Uniontown was Andrew Jackson, who used to keep the patrons at Hart's Tavern entertained with his lively stories.

In 1849, General Zachary Taylor traveled from Louisiana to Washington for his inauguration as President. He took a steamboat as far as Wheeling but made the rest of the journey by coach along the National Road. The night before the President-elect's party set out from Wheeling, there was a heavy sleet storm which left the landscape glittering like a snowy fairyland but made the turnpike nearly impassable.

The Presidential coach slipped and skidded from one side of the road to the other and once seemed on the verge of sliding right off an embankment into a narrow creek a hundred feet below. The members of the party escorting General Taylor were frightened out of their wits. They were sure that the new President was going to be killed. If he wasn't, they were almost as worried about what he would say to them for arranging such a nerve-racking journey.

When they finally reached the outskirts of Cumberland, the General's coach stopped and Taylor stepped out. His escorts leaped out of their own coaches prepared for an angry tongue-lashing. Instead, the new President greeted his relieved aides with a smile and said, "Gentlemen, I have to thank you; it has been the most wonderful ride, through the most beautiful scenery, that I have ever experienced."

An earlier President who did not enjoy his trip on the National Road was Martin Van Buren. Van Buren had been an outspoken foe of government road-building, a position not guaranteed to insure his popularity in Ohio, Indiana and Illinois. Soon after he left office, Van Buren made a trip to Indianapolis and on the way passed through Plainfield, Indiana.

When a celebrity came to town in those days, it was the custom to give him an ornate coach and a special driver and to set up huge flower-trimmed arches along his route. In Plainfield, the citizens were still angry over Van Buren's stand on the road issue. There were no triumphal arches on the town's main street. Moreover, some of the inhabitants enlisted the driver of the Presidential coach in a plot to gain revenge.

The young man "accidentally" bumped one wheel against a tree; the coach tipped over and its occupant was hurled into a mud puddle. As one historian described it, Martin Van Buren entered town " a bedraggled wreck of imported broadcloth, knee breeches, silk hose, satin waistcoat, high stock, magnificent beaver, and beruffled dignity." A small monument on Main Street marks the site of Plainfield's practical joke.

Martin Van Buren was not the only man in the country who opposed the National Road. Easterners complained about paying for a highway that benefitted only westerners, and many politicians questioned whether building roads was actually part of the federal government's job. To add more fuel to the fire, the road had turned out to be far more expensive than anyone had anticipated. The wheels of the heavy freight wagons and stagecoaches cut deep furrows into the macadam, and hoodlums destroyed the milestones. Engineers had estimated the original cost of the turnpike at $6000 a mile but apparently no one had thought to add in the extra expenses of keeping it repaired.

There were long arguments in Congress every time a bill to provide funds for the National Turnpike came up for debate, and by 1848 the government finally relinquished all responsibility for the highway and the Great National Turnpike became just another road.

The original sponsors of the road had hoped to see it reach as far as St. Louis. By the time it did, America had pushed farther west and her roads were stretching to keep up with her. The wagon trail soon went beyond St. Louis to Independence, Missouri.

Today Independence is famous as the home of former President Harry S. Truman and the site of the Harry S. Truman Library and Museum, but from about 1830 to 1850, it was the last stop for travelers setting out on the Santa Fe and Oregon Trails.

Both trails were already well established by the time the route out of Independence that grew into U.S. 40 began. It started with the discovery of gold in Colorado in 1859. Many gold-seekers, impatient to make their fortunes, bypassed the older roads and set out on a direct route across Kansas to Colorado. Their wagons and pack trains often carried signs saying "Pike's Peak or Bust."

Although the gold strike was almost a hundred miles from Pike's Peak, it was the only place that anyone had ever heard of in Colorado.

The first gold strike—Gregory Lode—spawned a settlement called Central City, which quickly became known as "the richest square mile on earth." Silver and lead were later found in Gregory Gulch, and when President Ulysses S. Grant visited Central City in 1873, he walked from his carriage to the Teller House hotel on a path made of solid silver bricks.

Denver, Colorado's capital, is east of Central City on Route 40. The town's first resident was a lone trapper who in 1857 built a wooden shack by the side of a creek. A year later the site had fifty more cabins and Colorado's first saloon. The 1859 gold rush attracted more settlers and within the next few decades, Denver grew into Colorado's most important city.

Some of the landmarks along U.S. 40 have been there long before the road, or even the country, began. Beyond Denver at Muddy Pass, for instance, the road crosses the Continental Divide—the ridge in the Rocky Mountains that separates the rivers flowing toward the Atlantic Ocean from those flowing toward the Pacific. Before leaving Colorado, the road passes Dinosaur National Monument, one of the largest fossil deposits in the world. Scientists there have unearthed the bones of dinosaurs estimated to be 140 million years old.

In 1776 a Spanish priest, Father Silvestre Velez de Escalante, mapped a trail through Colorado to the Great Salt Lake. Escalante had hoped to find a route that would connect the Spanish trading post at Santa Fe, New Mexico, with the newly established missions in California. His quest was unsuccessful, but U.S. 40's route across eastern Utah to Salt Lake City is almost identical to the path followed by Father Escalante and his party.

In California, the highway passes the site of one of the most frightening chapters in the story of the westward migration. In 1846 George Donner, an Illinois farmer, sold his lands and decided to move his family to California. Several of his relatives with their wives and children joined him, and a number of his neighbors came too. By the time they set out, the Donner Party numbered more than eighty people.

The emigrants followed the Oregon Trail as far as Wyoming. Then they foolishly took the advice of a book called *The Emigrants' Guide to Oregon and California.* It recommended a route that went "southwest to the Salt Lake; and thence continuing down to the Bay of San Francisco." It sounded simple, but what the author didn't mention—or perhaps didn't even know—was that this particular route led across some of the steepest peaks of the Sierra Nevada Mountains, peaks that were practically impassable once winter came.

The Donner party reached Lake's Crossing, now the city of Reno, Nevada, in late October. From there they set out across the Sierras. Just as they reached the pass through the mountains, the first of the winter storms overtook them. They built shelters, hoping to ride out the blizzard, but their food supplies gave out and they were forced to eat twigs and bark. Several members of the expedition soon died, several more went insane.

When a few volunteers set out to find help, half of them died along the way. The rest struggled across the snowy mountains and a month later arrived at an Indian village in California's Sacramento Valley. A rescue team finally made its way to the rest of the Donner party in February, 1847. By then only about forty of the original emigrants were left. Exhausted and weak from starvation, they told a harrowing tale of their fight for survival and confessed that they had been forced to eat the flesh of the other members of the party who died.

In 1865 a New York businessman named John Butterfield organized a passenger and express company to provide service between the Missouri River and Denver. The first stagecoaches followed a route that roughly parallels U.S. 40. The Butterfield Overland Dispatch was eventually bought out by Wells, Fargo and Company; Wells, Fargo, in turn, was driven out of business by the railroads.

The Iron Horse put a stop to much of the wagon traffic in the west, but it also brought prosperity to many of the towns along the old trails. One particularly busy stop was Abilene, Kansas. The first, and for awhile the most famous, of the west's cowtowns, Abilene was the northern terminus of the Chisholm Trail. Texas cowboys used to drive their cattle up along the trail and ship them by rail to market. In the late 1860's, Abilene had as many dance halls, saloons and outlaws as any town in the west. One of the many sheriffs who tried to enforce law and order there was the former Indian scout and soldier, "Wild Bill" Hickok.

Abilene's prosperity declined around 1872 when Dodge City succeeded it as "Queen of the Cowtowns," but the city is noted today as the boyhood home of President Dwight D. Eisenhower. The Eisenhower Center includes the house in which he lived, the museum with his Presidential papers and personal mementoes, and the Memorial Chapel in which he is buried.

U.S. 40 is a combination of the old National Road, the prospectors' trail to Colorado and the roads to Utah, Nevada and California that grew out of it. Linked together, they have become a 3000-mile-long highway that reaches from Atlantic City, New Jersey, to San Francisco. It is a more modern road than its predecessors, but travelers on it can still find many reminders of its historic past.

Two of the original bridges from the National Road are not far from Route 40. One, the Casselman Bridge in Garrett, Maryland, was built in 1813. At the time, its stone arch was the largest in the United States. Another bridge from the old turnpike has been preserved in a roadside park near Old Washington, Ohio.

George Washington's camp at Fort Necessity is now a National Park near Uniontown, Pennsylvania. A plaque at the site reads:

HERE JULY 3RD, 1754, LIEUTENANT COLONEL GEORGE WASHINGTON FOUGHT HIS FIRST BATTLE WHICH MARKED THE BEGINNING OF THE FRENCH AND INDIAN WAR IN AMERICA AND STARTED THE SEVEN YEARS WAR IN EUROPE.

The Casselman Bridge.

Not far away is the grave of General Edward Braddock. More than fifty years after his death, a party of workmen repairing the road dug up a skeleton and some military buttons. They moved the remains to a site under a large tree and marked the spot with a crude sign. In 1913 a permanent stone marker was placed at the General's grave.

Ebenezer Zane's family name is still commemorated in Zanesville, Ohio, and at Wheeling a plaque marks the site of Fort Henry, which he defended against the British in the American Revolution.

The Madonna of the Trail, at Springfield, Ohio.

In St. Louis, a soaring stainless steel arch, the Jefferson National Expansion Memorial, commemorates the days when Missouri was the gateway to the west.

In Nevada, tourists often visit Central City's mining museum or attend a performance at its recently refurbished Opera House.

At Donner Pass in the Sierra Nevada Mountains, a marker by the side of the road pays tribute to the sufferings of the members of the Donner expedition.

But perhaps the most familiar monument along U.S. 40 is the Madonna of the Trails, the well-known statue of a pioneer mother with a baby in her arms and a small boy clinging to her homespun skirts. There are twelve of these memorials at various spots along the route of the early westerners. They are fitting reminders of the families who braved the country's first turnpike and helped America grow up.

8

U.S. 101 El Camino Real—
The Spanish Mission Trail

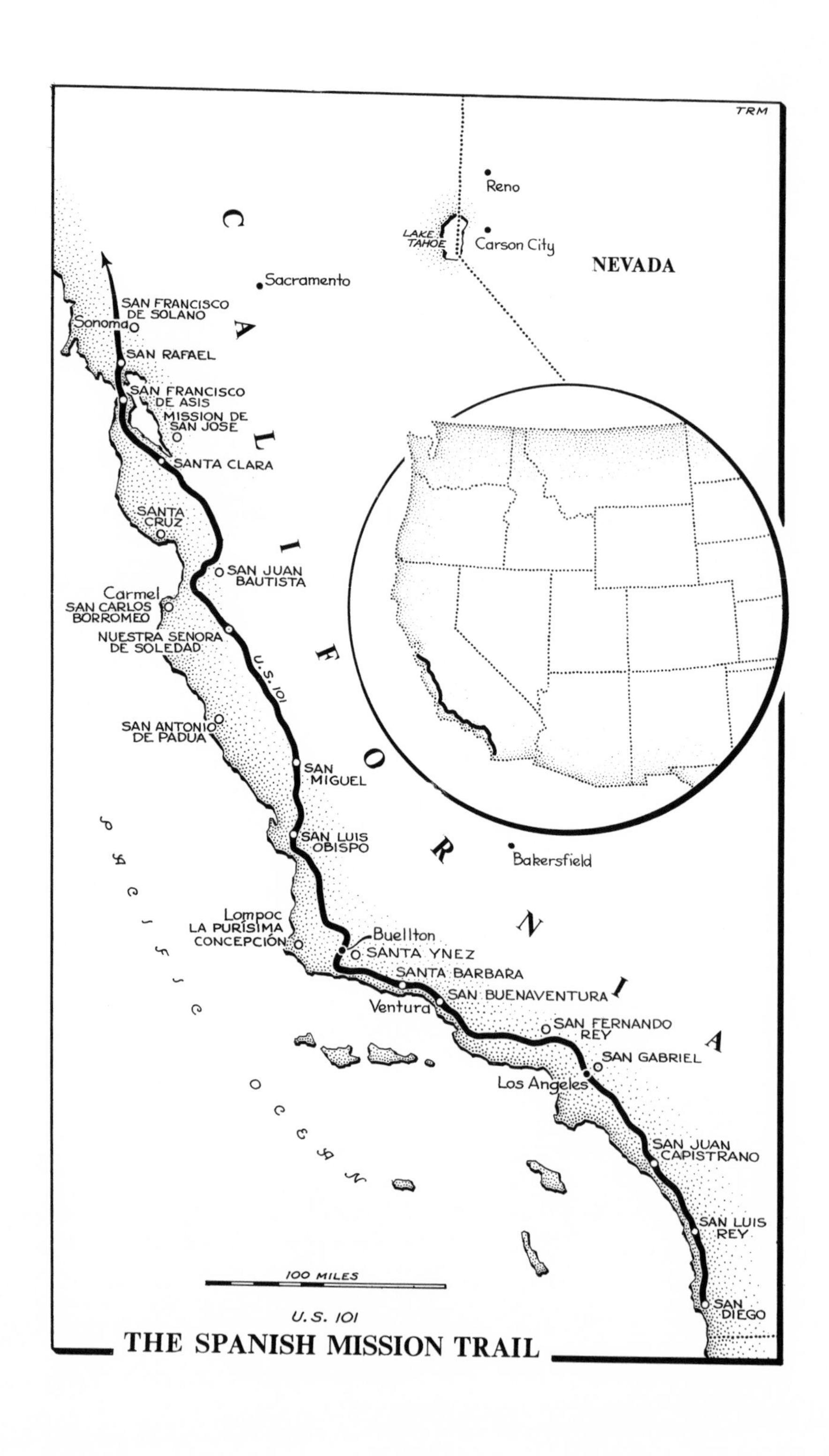

THE SPANISH MISSION TRAIL

The highway markers along U.S. 101 in California read like a Spanish litany of saints—San Diego, Santa Barbara, San Luis Obispo, San Jose, Santa Clara, San Francisco. The names come from the early Spanish missions, and the road that connects them was for more than a hundred years *El Camino Real*—the Royal Highway of the Kings of Spain.

Then, as now, the road started in San Diego, the city where California itself began. The site was first visited by the Spanish explorer Juan Cabrillo in 1542, and received its name from another seafarer, Sebastian Vizcaino, sixty years later. Vizcaino also christened a number of other places along the California coastline. San Diego and Santa Barbara honored the saints on whose days they had been sighted; Carmel was suggested by a Carmelite monk who accompanied the voyagers; and Monterey was named after the Count of Monte Rey, the Spanish Viceroy in Mexico who had sponsored the expedition.

Vizcaino returned with tales of tall mountains, friendly Indians and fabulous harbors—particularly the one at Monterey—but it was not until 1769 that Captain Gaspar de Portola was ordered to lead a march north and take possession of the land in the name of God and the King of Spain. With him marched a Franciscan missionary priest named Father Junipero Serra.

Their initial stop in Alta California—as the Spaniards called the northern stretch of the Pacific coast—was San Diego. There, on the 16th of July, Father Serra founded his first mission. He remained behind to supervise its construction while Portola and his soldiers continued north in search of Vizcaino's famous port of

Monterey. Their line of march was almost identical to the route that has since become California's most important north and south highway. Opening the new road, however, was the pathfinders' only accomplishment. Portola's men returned sick and weary from their long march, without ever finding the famed harbor of Monterey.

When a second expedition was sent out the following year, Father Junipero Serra went with it. This time the explorers reached Monterey and the dedicated Franciscan founded his second mission, San Carlos Borromeo, at nearby Carmel. Father Serra's plan was to establish a string of missions between Monterey and San Diego, each within one day's traveling distance of the next.

Serra started the chain a year later by marching seventy-five miles out of Carmel to found a third mission at San Antonio. One of his friars at San Diego began a fourth at San Gabriel, and in 1772 Serra started the fifth, San Luis Obispo. It was named for St. Louis, the Bishop of Toulouse, because a pair of volcanic peaks nearby reminded Serra of a bishop's mitre.

The missionary priests hoped to convert the Indians to Christianity and to teach them farming, weaving and animal husbandry as well. The neophytes, as the converts were called, lived and worked at the missions, so each site was a village in itself. Until the friars taught the neophytes to make the more durable adobe, the buildings were simple wooden structures. Their original thatched roofs were abandoned after a series of disastrous fires and replaced by tile that was devised by the priests at San Luis Obispo and quickly adopted by all the other missions.

The route of Captain Gaspar de Portola's soldiers soon became a well-worn trail as the monks in their dark robes and leather sandals traveled back and forth between their settlements. Each mission also had a presidio—a small garrison of soldiers. One of the soldiers usually accompanied the priests on their travels to protect them from the grizzly bears that roamed the woods and to keep an eye out for Indians who sometimes hid along the cliffs

Father Junipero Serra. (The Bettmann Archive)

above the trail and pelted unwary passersby with stones and arrows.

The most faithful traveler on the mission circuit was Father

Junipero Serra. His missions stretched along a four-hundred-mile road that started with the original one at San Diego and ran all the way up to San Francisco. Father Serra visited them all regularly, sometimes traveling by mule, more often on foot. He made his last tour in 1783. By then he was almost seventy years old and in failing health. When he returned to his headquarters at Carmel, he smiled weakly at his priests and neophytes and announced that he had come home to die.

Serra died the following August. By then there were nine missions along El Camino Real. His successor, Father Fermin Francisco de Lasuen, founded nine more, making a total of eighteen, the exact number Serra had originally planned. Several more were subsequently added, the last completed in 1823.

By then the mission road was California's main highway. Trappers and traders, soldiers and even a visiting British sailor, Captain Frederick William Beechey of His Majesty's Ship *Blossom*, traveled along it. The officer was impressed by the "parklike scenery," but there was little else to see except farmland, livestock and an occasional mud hut inhabited by half-naked Indians.

A few ranches along the road belonged to sons and grandsons of Gaspar de Portola's soldiers who had stayed behind in California. But only at the missions could the traveler always be certain of finding hospitality. Food, lodging and a fresh horse were offered without charge. Often the latest gossip and a few games of Spanish whist were included in the bargain.

Since the founding of the first one, San Diego, in 1769, the missions had grown into huge and extremely prosperous establishments. San Luis Rey was a cluster of striking white buildings that resembled a Moorish palace. Aptly named the King of the Missions, it provided a home for some three thousand neophytes, and its land holdings offered pastures for more than twice that number of cattle. Santa Barbara, the Queen of the Missions, was almost as rich and its twin-towered church was considered even more beautiful. Santa Clara was famous for the excellence of its fruits, and San Antonio de Padua for its fine vegetables. San Gabriel boasted the first vineyards ever planted in California; in a good year they yielded over a thousand barrels of wine and several hundred casks of brandy.

Occasionally a horseman with news from Mexico or a message from one of the other missions came galloping along the trail, but more often, the King's Highway was a sleepy country road disturbed only by the lowing of cattle and the tolling of the mission bells.

The first signs of change on El Camino Real came when a fleet of New England merchant ships arrived in California in the 1820's. Their captains were looking for sea otter pelts to trade in the Orient, but it did not take long for them to realize that other equally valuable skins were to be had in California—hides from the cattle of the missions and ranches along the Royal Road.

The shrewd New England hide agents roamed up and down the road, bargaining with the missionaries and rancheros. Soon cartloads full of the precious hides—which became known as "California bank notes"—were lumbering up along the mission trail to be loaded onto waiting ships and sent not only to Boston but to England and South America as well.

The tranquility of the old trail was disturbed still further when in 1833 the Mexican government announced that the missions were to be disbanded. Half of the lands, livestock and supplies would be taken over by the state, the other half was to be divided among the Indians. The Franciscan missionaries could remain in California, but they would function only as parish priests.

The secularization of the missions might have been a good idea, but it was carried out by hasty, incompetent and sometimes dishonest administrators. Many Indians, helpless without their priestly guides, refused to accept the lands they were given. Enterprising rancheros promptly stepped in and bought them at ridiculously low prices. The Indians ended up as hired hands. Some of them had to resort to begging along El Camino Real.

Meanwhile the ranches along the highway grew larger and more splendid. Many covered as much as fifty thousand acres.

The whitewashed adobe houses with their tile roofs and iron-grilled windows were furnished with fine silverware and imported paintings and rugs. Extra buildings were needed to accommodate the scores of ranch hands and house servants who tended the huge establishments. For the rancheros, at least, the Royal Road seemed to be paved with gold.

The missions, once the main centers of activity along the highway, fell into almost total decay, but small villages—pueblos—began to spring up near the same sites. Each was built Spanish style, with a town square flanked by one or two stores, a jailhouse and a church. Other towns grew up at smaller settlements in between the missions. One, Nuestra Senora de Los Angeles de Porciuncula, had received its name from Gaspar de Portola. The town has since grown much larger and its name much shorter. Modern Los Angeles now sprawls over 463 square miles and has a population that comes close to the three million mark.

The Spanish flavor of El Camino Real began to change in 1848. The war with Mexico, which ended in that year, made California an American possession. Not long afterward, gold was discovered at Sutter's Mill, and Americans by the thousands began pouring into the newly acquired state.

Many of the forty-niners took the route through Texas and across the mountains to San Diego. From there they trudged up the Coast Highway—as the Americans now called El Camino Real—and found their way to the gold mines in the northern part of the state. Conestoga wagons became a common sight on the highway. Most of the traffic was heading north and anyone coming from the opposite direction was immediately stopped and pressed for information about the vast treasure that was to be found at the end of the dusty trail.

The population of California began to grow at an astonishing rate, but unfortunately the state soon became as well known for its lawlessness as it was for its promises of wealth. Thieves and murderers invaded the state in droves. They found so many of their victims along the Coast Highway that it became an unwritten rule that no one traveled the route alone.

A postal employee who was brave enough to risk the journey was attacked by a band of cutthroats who chased him down the road and across open fields for over fifty miles. He spent two days eluding his pursuers and finally escaped under cover of darkness and hid in an abandoned barn. When daylight came, he discovered that he was sharing his refuge with five corpses—the bodies of an emigrant family who had been robbed and murdered by another band of highwaymen.

The Coast Highway became busier but not much safer with the founding of Wells, Fargo and Company. The owners of the firm, Henry Wells and William G. Fargo, already operated the highly successful American Express Company in the east. In 1852 they opened a western branch with headquarters in San Francisco. The company offered express service to California's remote mining camps, bringing letters and packages into the mountains and shipments of gold and silver out. The Wells, Fargo wagons also carried passengers, and their operations soon extended beyond the mining country to the rest of the Pacific coast and to other western territories as well.

Before the stagecoach service could begin on the Coast Highway, it was necessary to initiate a few repairs on the old road. The towns of Los Angeles and Santa Barbara agreed to grade and fill the seventy-five miles of ruts between them. San Francisco and San Jose were joined by a forty-mile turnpike covered with planks. Ferries were replaced by bridges, bogs were filled in, crude milestones were set down at several points, and inns, or "mile" houses, began to appear beside them.

Despite these improvements, one stagecoach company felt obliged to warn its passengers: "Don't imagine for a moment that you are going on a picnic." Anyone who had made the trip knew otherwise. Some parts of the road ran along rocky cliffs, others came perilously close to the ocean. One coach tipped over on the road near Santa Barbara and passengers and baggage landed in the Pacific surf. In addition, many of the California creeks looked deceptively shallow. On more than one occasion, passengers had to be lassoed and dragged from their sinking stagecoaches by lariat-toting hands from the ranches along the way.

Crime along the road was cut to some extent by vigilantes—armed citizens who acted as self-appointed policemen and occasionally proved to be as much of a menace as the criminals they were supposed to be apprehending. But the stagecoaches along the Coast Highway still offered a great temptation to bandits. They carried the United States Mail which often contained cash. In addition, the passengers could usually be counted on for a generous haul of jewelry, coins, and other valuables.

The most notorious and colorful of the stagecoach robbers was a masked bandit named Black Bart. In eight years he held up at least twenty-eight drivers, usually leaving behind a piece of paper with a few lines of verse which he signed Black Bart the Po8—his code name for poet. Black Bart had two rules: he never killed and he never stole from women. He was finally apprehended in San Francisco, where he worked as a respectable mining engineer, but his name is commemorated at Black Bart Rock, which stands near the Coast Highway about a hundred miles above the Golden Gate.

Of the many towns that grew up along California's Coast Highway, the most exciting was—and still is—San Francisco. In 1846 the USS *Portsmouth* sailed into the harbor of the tiny mission town and Captain John B. Montgomery raised the American flag over the town square. The discovery of gold at Sutter's Mill, three years later, brought a flood of people into San Francisco. Prospectors stopped on their way to or from the mining camps and pitched their tents on its hillsides. Behind the miners came the businessmen—dealers in tobacco, workclothes and mining equipment—and bankers and brokers to see that the wealth of the gold fields was put to good use.

For the first half century of its existence as an American city,

REWARD!

WELLS, FARGO & CO.'S EXPRESS BOX, CON-
taining $160 in Gold Notes, was robbed this morning, by one man, on the route from Sonora to Milton, near top of the Hill, between the river and Copperopolis.

$250

And one-fourth of any money recovered, will be paid
for arrest and conviction of the robber.

JOHN J. VALENTINE,
General Sup't.

San Francisco, July 27, 1875.

Black Bart, and a contemporary reward poster. (Courtesy Wells Fargo Bank)

San Francisco was a reckless town, best known for the string of saloons and gambling houses along its Barbary Coast. In April 1906, the former mission was hit by a tremendous earthquake and a fire that raged for three days. Most of the city's downtown section, including the infamous Barbary Coast, was destroyed. Rebuilt during the next decade, San Francisco became a more respectable, but still glamorous city. Tourists love its steep hills, fine restaurants and clanging cable cars.

Some of the names you hear in San Francisco—Stanford, Huntington, Crocker—are the names of railroad magnates who made their fortunes building railroad lines to connect northern and southern California and to join the state with the rest of the cities across the country. Traffic along the Coast Highway diminished considerably with the coming of the railroads in the 1860's, but the railroads also made the first attempts to lure eastern tourists out to California.

Huge resort hotels, advertised as the height of luxury, were built to attract them. In Santa Barbara, The Arlington, which boasted elevators and gas lighting, played host to three Presidents, Benjamin Harrison, William McKinley and Theodore Roosevelt. San Francisco's Palace Hotel was equally famous, although when Rudyard Kipling stayed there he was appalled to see the desk clerk picking his teeth in front of the guests.

To impress the eastern tourists and to satisfy the complaints of local residents, a few parts of the Coast Highway, mainly around the cities, had been widened and paved. Unfortunately, much of the work that had been done on the road was completely undone by the great San Francisco earthquake of 1906. The quake destroyed over 25,000 buildings and killed more than four hundred people. The highway, too, bore signs of the disaster. In some places it was twisted and buckled into outlandish shapes. In others, crevices over twenty feet deep yawned across the roadway.

By the time the road through San Francisco was rebuilt, people who lived along other parts of the highway began to demand improvements. The automobile was gradually replacing the horse and buggy and drivers complained about damaging their tires and engines on the rocky path. In some places desperate car owners actually went out and repaired the road themselves.

Another source of complaint were the highway markers—or lack of them. There were rarely any signs to indicate how far a motorist had come, where he was, or how much farther he had to go. In addition, during the rainy season, the drivers were constantly paying local farmers and ranchers to haul their cars out of the mud. A few irate motorists insisted that the farmers took their money in the daytime and then returned at night to pour more water into the holes.

By 1925 the Coast Highway finally became smoother, wider and safer. By then the United States government decided that the nation's highways deserved a coherent marking system. Signs were erected and all federal roads were given numbers. East-west highways were numbered evenly, starting from the Canadian border. North-south highways were given odd numbers, starting at the Atlantic shoreline. Under the new system, California's Coast Highway became U.S. 101.

The Coast Highway had been pushed up into Oregon and Washington soon after the California gold rush. Its two sections were officially joined with the opening of San Francisco's Golden Gate Bridge in 1937. To the old mission trail were added three hundred miles of the spectacular Redwood Highway, and U.S. 101 became a continuous thoroughfare from San Diego to the old fur trading post of Astoria, Oregon, and on into Canada. The San Diego to San Francisco section has since become a multi-lane freeway where cars zoom by at ninety or a hundred miles an hour.

In recent years, the missions which were responsible for the growth of El Camino Real have been restored or rebuilt. Still used as churches, they are also among the favorite attractions for the thousands of tourists who visit California each year. Each has some special claim to fame.

The church at San Diego joyfully commemorates its founding

in 1769 with the Festival of the Bells on the Sunday nearest the 16th of July. San Juan Capistrano has become known for its migration of swallows who fly away each fall on October 23rd, the Feast of St. John, and return faithfully each spring on March 19th, the Feast of St. Joseph. At San Gabriel, the original mission still stands. It dates back to 1791 and is the third oldest structure in the state. Even older, however, is the lovely church of San Carlos Borromeo at Carmel, where Father Junipero Serra is buried. The devoted monk succeeded in giving California her first Christians, but he might be surprised to learn that he created her first highway as well.

9

U.S. 50 The Santa Fe Trail and the Route of the Pony Express

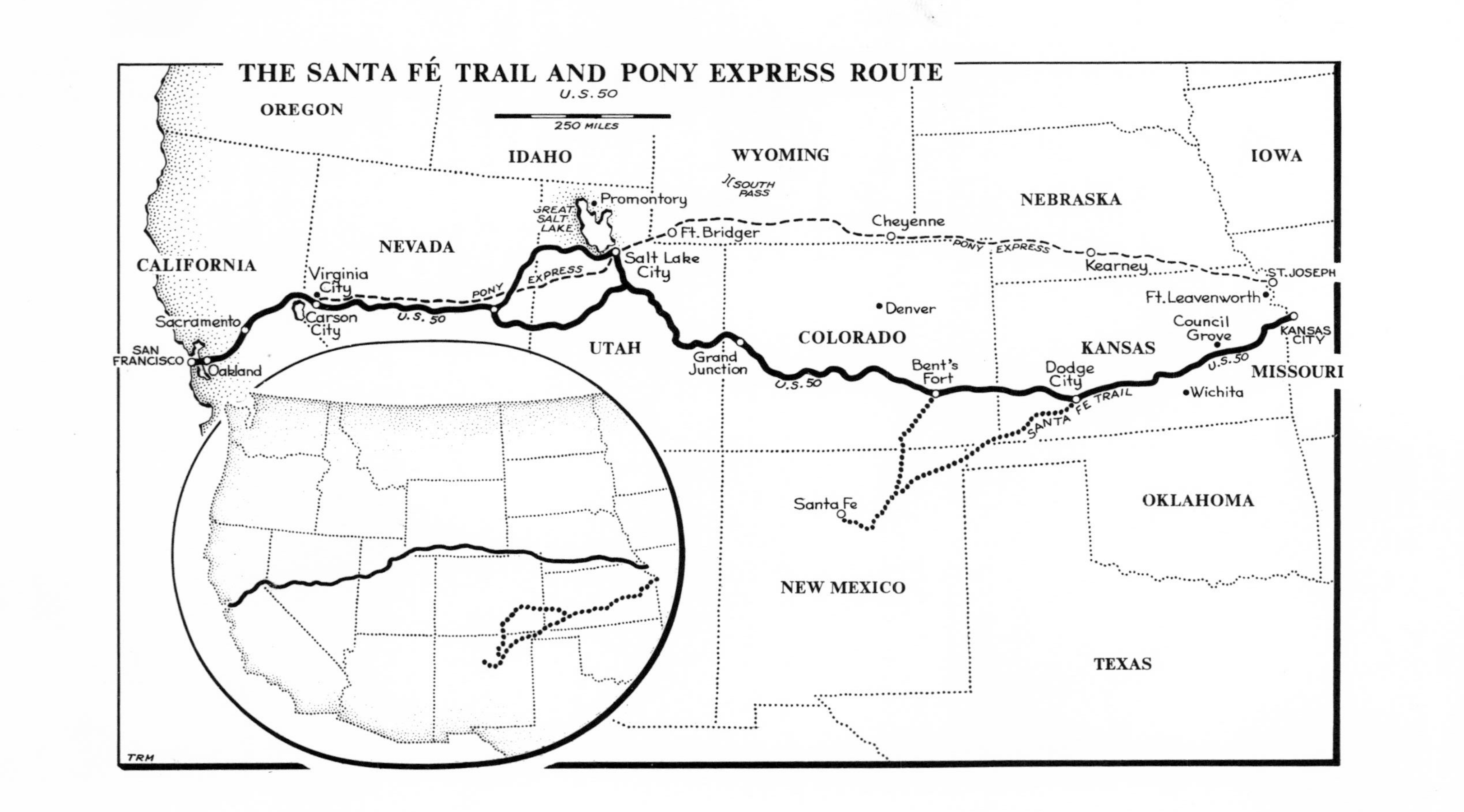
THE SANTA FÉ TRAIL AND PONY EXPRESS ROUTE
U.S. 50
250 MILES
OREGON
IDAHO
WYOMING
IOWA
SOUTH PASS
NEBRASKA
Promontory
GREAT SALT LAKE
NEVADA
CALIFORNIA
Ft. Bridger
Cheyenne
PONY EXPRESS
Kearney
Salt Lake City
ST. JOSEPH
Virginia City
Ft. Leavenworth
Denver
Sacramento
Carson City
U.S. 50
Council Grove
COLORADO
KANSAS CITY
SAN FRANCISCO
Oakland
UTAH
KANSAS
Grand Junction
Bent's Fort
Dodge City
MISSOURI
Wichita
SANTA FE TRAIL
Santa Fe
OKLAHOMA
NEW MEXICO
TEXAS
TRM

From Ocean City, Maryland, to Kansas City, Missouri, U.S. 50 is a fairly ordinary highway, but the section of it that runs from Kansas City to San Francisco is rich in history. It follows part of the Santa Fe Trail and part of an early trail to California, parallels the route of the Pony Express and passes through two of the wildest towns in the old west—Carson City, Nevada, and Dodge City, Kansas.

Long before the road to Santa Fe was opened, American traders had been dreaming of the fortunes they could make there. The city was noted for its rich silver and fine wool, but it was totally lacking in manufactured goods like tools and knives. Santa Fe was obviously a trader's paradise, but it was also a foreign city, part of Spain's empire in Mexico, and the Spaniards were determined not to share its wealth with their neighbors to the north. The few Americans who made the trip to Santa Fe were hurled into prison and the goods they brought to trade were confiscated.

In 1821 the Mexicans overthrew their Spanish masters, and word reached the United States that foreigners would now be welcome in Santa Fe. Several traders immediately set out for the city; the first to arrive was William Becknell and the route he followed became the main route of the Santa Fe Trail.

Becknell left from Franklin, Missouri, in September 1821. He reached Santa Fe on November 16, traded his goods and returned home forty-eight days later. The townspeople who turned out to meet him gaped when they saw the torrent of silver dollars that rained out on the ground when his saddlebags were opened.

One woman, whose brother went along on Becknell's expedition, had given him $60 to pay for his supplies. He made such a profit on the venture that he returned $900 to her.

Other traders quickly followed Becknell's trail, leading their pack horses across Kansas and Colorado and then turning south toward New Mexico. Most of them made the trip without mishap, but a few lost their way and narrowly escaped death from starvation and thirst. One trading party was so desperate for water that they cut off the ears of their mules and drank the blood.

The traders boasted about the hardships of the trail. They were tough outdoorsmen, used to—in fact, eager for—adventure. But there was one Missouri man, Senator Thomas Hart Benton, who was determined to see the road made safe.

Benton's home state was, at that point in American history, the last outpost of civilization. Beyond the Missouri River there was nothing but a vast frontier. Benton was certain that the United States would one day conquer that frontier. He even foresaw a time when the nation would stretch from the Atlantic coastline to the shores of the Pacific.

Although many people found Benton's dream of westward expansion absurd, the Senator continued to take advantage of every opportunity to extend his country's influence on the North American continent.

At Benton's suggestion, Congress passed a bill authorizing a government survey of the Santa Fe Trail. It was signed into law by President James Monroe in 1825. The bill provided for an appropriation of $30,000. $10,000 was to be spent on mapping and marking the trail; the rest was to be used to pay the Indians for the right to pass through their territory.

A government commissioner met with the chiefs of the Osage tribes at Council Grove, Kansas, about 76 miles from the present U.S. 50. The men met under an oak tree and smoked a pipe of peace. They agreed that each tribe was to be given eight hundred dollars in silver and goods in return for their promise to allow traders to pass without harm. Unfortunately the commissioner neglected to make similar agreements with two other tribes—the Pawnees and the Comanches—who also had a claim to land near the trail.

Caravans along the road to Santa Fe were not attacked by Indians very often, but when they were, the Pawnees or the Comanches were invariably involved. Their main interest was in stealing. They would circle a wagon train, shrieking and waving blankets until they drove off all the horses and mules. The traders, left to walk, soon abandoned their goods and the Indians succeeded in getting both a new supply of livestock and some valuable trade goods as well.

Another favorite tactic of the Comanches was the death circle. After stampeding the white men's horses, the Indians would form a circle just out of range of the traders' rifle fire. Then they would ride around and around the stranded white men, finally attacking them when they were too tired and hungry to resist.

It took only a few such encounters with the Comanches before the caravans began hiring guards to protect them. The man they usually called upon was Kit Carson. Carson was the leader of a small band of hunters and guides who made their headquarters at Bent's Fort in Colorado and divided their time between hunting buffalo and protecting travelers on the Santa Fe Trail.

The Indians never bothered a caravan that was guarded by Carson Men. Six of them, including Carson himself, had once been attacked by a Comanche war party not far from Bent's Fort. Thinking quickly, Carson leaped from his mule, slashed its throat and ordered his men to do the same thing. Then they crawled beneath the dead animals, where the Indians' arrows could not hit them.

When the Indians tried to charge, the smell of fresh blood frightened their ponies off. The next step was the Comanches' death circle, but again Carson outwitted the braves. Knowing that the Comanches were extremely superstitious, he began shouting insults at their medicine man. He told him that he had

Kit Carson. (Culver Pictures)

his own medicine that he would scatter on the wind when darkness came. He vowed it would wipe the warriors out.

The medicine man, determined to show his own powers, began chanting, waving charms and dancing. After whipping the braves into a frenzy, he led them in a full scale charge against the Carson Men. Carson himself went out to meet them; he killed the medicine man with a single shot from his rifle and then hurled himself to the ground seconds before the warriors unleashed a storm of flying arrows. The Indian ponies again panicked at the smell of the mules' blood and retreated. At that point, Carson leaped to his feet unharmed. The Comanches, certain that their arrows had hit him, were astonished to find him still alive. They raced off across the desert, loath to risk any further encounters with a man who possessed such amazing powers.

William Becknell had established the original trail to Santa Fe, the same one U.S. 50 follows so closely. Later traders developed short cuts, but Becknell's route remained the most popular, especially after Bent's Fort was built as a way station. The fort was on the north shore of the Arkansas River about seven miles from the present city of La Junta, Colorado. It was built around 1832 by three brothers, Charles, William and George Bent, and for a few years, it flew the only American flag west of the Missouri River.

A huge building with adobe walls fifteen feet high and four feet thick, Bent's Fort had its own arsenal, workshops and warehouses. Caravans stopped there on their way back and forth to New Mexico. They could trade with the friendly Cheyenne Indians, replenish their supplies, find shelter for the night and dine on buffalo meat supplied by the Carson Men. Today the fort is a national historic site.

The first travelers on the Santa Fe Trail left from the steamboat landing at Franklin, Missouri. Their trade goods were sent by boat from the east and they could easily be unloaded there and transferred to wagons or packhorses. Franklin was a prosperous settlement until in 1828 floodwaters from the Missouri River drowned the town's hopes in a sea of mud. Eventually it was rebuilt and became New Franklin, but by then the terminus of the Santa Fe trail had moved farther up the Missouri to Independence.

Independence began to lose its importance as an outfitting point around 1845 when a few trading companies started using an Indian trading post a short distance away called Westport. In Independence there was a long dirt road between the steamboat landing and the village. When the spring rains came, it often took days to haul the goods from the dock to the wagon trains. At Westport, there were no such delays. Moreover, there was plenty of land on which the wagon trains could assemble and enough grass for their teams to graze on while they waited for the journey to begin. Westport and its neighbor, Westport Landing, became the new departure points for overland travelers. They grew even busier over the years and are now merged into Kansas City, Missouri's second largest city.

The Santa Fe Trail had always been a commercial route, but during the Mexican War it became a military road. In 1846 an army under the command of Colonel Stephen Watts Kearny marched from Fort Leavenworth, just north of Kansas City, to New Mexico and conquered Santa Fe without firing a shot. Two years later the treaty of Guadalupe-Hidalgo ended the war and gave the United States New Mexico and California. The trading caravans not only increased, but a stagecoach line was organized to carry mail and passengers. The Missouri *Commonwealth* described the service:

> "The stages are gotten up in elegant style, and are each arranged to convey eight passengers. The bodies are beautifully painted and made water-tight, with a view of using them as boats in ferrying streams. The team consists of six mules to each coach. The mail is guarded by eight men, armed as follows: Each man has at his side, fastened in the stage, one Colt's revolving rifle, in a holster below, one of Colt's long revolvers, and in his belt a small Colt's revolver, besides a hunting knife, so that these eight men are ready, in case of at-

tack, to discharge 136 shots without having to reload. This is equal to a small army armed as in ancient times, and from the look of the escort, ready as they were either for offensive or defensive warfare with the savages, we have no fear for the safety of the mails."

Despite its supposed dangers, the Santa Fe Trail continued to be one of the busiest commercial routes in the west. In 1843 some $450,000 worth of goods was transported over it. By 1855 the figure had risen to five million dollars' worth. The road's importance did not diminish until the Atchison, Topeka and Santa Fe Railroad was completed in 1880 and took away most of its traffic.

In 1848, the news of a gold strike in California brought a stampede of easterners to the Pacific coast. They came by various routes; a few took the Santa Fe Trail as far as Bent's Fort and then headed north to the Mormon settlement at Salt Lake City. From there they picked up the California Trail through northern Nevada into San Francisco. A detour on this trail, known as the Carson Branch, led into the Washoe Valley in Nevada. The discovery of the Comstock Silver Lode in the Washoe Valley in 1859 quickly turned this rarely used detour into a well-traveled road. Would-be prospectors came from two directions, southwest from Salt Lake City and east over the Sierra Nevadas, from Sacramento and San Francisco.

The first mining camp was at Virginia City, where prospectors had found the strange "blue dirt" that turned out to be silver ore worth over a dollar an ounce. In its heyday, Virginia City had four banks, six churches, an opera house, 110 saloons and the only elevator between Chicago and San Francisco. But the Comstock mines began to peter out less than two decades after their discovery and Virginia City's population dwindled over the years from 30,000 to a mere 500. Today the city exists mainly for tourists anxious to visit one of the west's most publicized ghost towns.

Carson City, Nevada's capital, is another former mining camp founded in the days of the Comstock Lode. The site was called Eagle Ranch originally, but it was later renamed for Kit Carson.

One of the most interesting buildings in Carson City today is the former United States Mint. It was opened in 1866 when Nevada ranked a close second to California in the production of precious metals and the San Francisco Mint was so overburdened that a second one was needed. The mint was closed after the decline of the Comstock mines and the building now houses the Nevada State Museum. Its many fascinating exhibits include a three-hundred-foot-long mine tunnel complete with hoisting, drilling and blasting equipment.

Another memento of Nevada's mining days is the Sutro Tunnel, about a mile north of U.S. 50 and about two miles east of the town of Dayton. The tunnel, in its day one of the engineering wonders of the world, was built by Adolph Sutro. In 1864 Sutro conceived the idea of digging under the Comstock Lode to provide drainage and ventilation and make the mines safe to work in. Sutro's tunnel cost over two million dollars, but by the time it was finished in 1878, the Comstock mines were on the brink of exhaustion and it was never used.

The "fifty-niners" spurred the growth of several cities in Nevada, but the main stops along Route 50 in California date back to the days of the "forty-niners." Placerville was in the heart of the gold country. Marshall Gold Discovery State Historic Park, the site where James Marshall discovered the precious metal in 1848, is only eight miles out of town. The first year of mining produced ten million dollars' worth of gold and made everyone in Placerville rich.

Because the miners were often preyed on by bandits, a vigilante group was formed to hunt down and punish outlaws in the vicinity. The self-appointed lawmen did their job so efficiently that Placerville soon became known as Hangtown. The Old Hangtown Bell, used to call out the vigilantes when a manhunt was being organized, still stands in Post Office Park on Bedford Avenue. Another bell near St. Patrick's Church was used to announce church services and was made from silver donated by miners.

Sacramento, which is also on U.S. 50, was settled in 1839 by Captain John A. Sutter and a group of Swiss immigrants. They raised wheat, milled flour and ran a shipping line down the Sacramento River to San Francisco. The colony collapsed when Sutter's partner, James Marshall, discovered gold at Coloma, about fifty miles away. The settlers quickly deserted Sutter's Fort to become miners in the nearby hills. A year after the gold rush, however, a new town, Sacramento City, was laid out. Within a year it had 10,000 residents and in 1854 it became the capital of California.

In the turbulent years before the Civil War, the United States government was anxious to keep in close touch with its westernmost state. Telegraph service was already available between Washington and St. Joseph, Missouri, but wires had yet to be installed beyond St. Joseph to California. When the government began looking for a communications system to bridge the distance, William Russell, a partner in the western freight firm of Russell, Majors and Waddell, came up with an idea. He proposed using fast horses, ridden in relays, to deliver mail to California within ten days.

The route Russell mapped out was 1966 miles long. It paralleled the Oregon Trail west as far as Salt Lake City. From there it followed modern U.S. 50 around the southern end of the Great Salt Lake through Carson City and Placerville to Sacramento.

The Pony Express riders were selected, like today's jockeys, for their slender builds; their horses were fleet-footed Indian mounts. Relay stations were built at 15-mile intervals. At each station the riders had two minutes in which to dismount, transfer their saddlebags to fresh ponies, remount and take off again. After several such stops, the riders handed the mail over to relief riders and the chain continued. Russell's mail service made its first run on April 3, 1860. Riders left simultaneously from Sacramento and St. Joseph, and the mail from each direction reached its destination within the ten days Russell had promised.

The Pony Express was abandoned in October 1861, when the

The Pony Express. (Courtesy Wells Fargo Bank)

cross-country telegraph was finally completed. In the brief year and a half of its operations, however, the riders had more than their share of mishaps and adventures. One rider was caught in a buffalo stampede; another got stuck in the mud and spent hours fighting off wolves until someone came to his rescue. But the Pony Express's most glorious feat was bringing Abraham Lincoln's inaugural address to Sacramento in February, 1861. The United States was periously close to a civil war and the whole country was waiting to see whether California would side with the north or the south. The final decision depended heavily on what the new President said in his inaugural speech.

The Pony Express was determined to get the President's words to California even faster than usual. Russell shortened the distance between relay stations to ten miles and hired only his fastest riders for the job. One, "Pony Bob" Haslam, was chosen for the worst stretch—120 miles of western Nevada filled with rampaging Paiutes.

Soon after he took off, Pony Bob was attacked by the Indians. Their horses, as swift as his own, had been stolen from one of the Pony Express relay stations. Haslam finally managed to outdistance them, but not without being hit. His arm was pierced by an arrow and another arrow tore through his jaw, breaking the bone and knocking out five of his teeth. At the next relay station, Pony Bob had the arrow cut from his arm; he put a clean rag in his mouth to staunch the flow of blood from his shattered jaw, and continued on his way. By the time he reached the last station, his face was swollen beyond recognition and his arm was puffed up to three times its normal size. But he had performed the superhuman feat of covering 120 miles in eight hours, changing horses a dozen times. Just seven days and seventeen hours after Lincoln's address had arrived in St. Joseph by wire, another rider brought it into Sacramento.

The speech prompted California to remain in the Union, but many of the state's inhabitants remained strongly pro-southern. One night in 1864 a band of robbers held up two stagecoaches at

Bullion Bend, about fifteen miles from Placerville on Route 50. The bandit leader gave both drivers receipts for the stolen cash. Made out to Wells, Fargo and Company, they stated that he planned to use the money for outfitting California recruits to fight for the Confederacy in the battle between the states.

As the telegraph replaced the Pony Express, so the railroads replaced the stagecoaches and wagons that had carried passengers and freight across the country. The first transcontinental rail line was completed in 1869 when Union Pacific tracks pushing east from Sacramento and west from Omaha met in the mountains north of the Great Salt Lake at Promontory Point, Utah. The second major line in the west was the Atchison, Topeka and Santa Fe. It closely followed the old Santa Fe Trail and some of the stops along the trail became important railroad junctions. One, Dodge City, was built only a few miles from a United States army post, Fort Dodge. It was laid out by railroad construction crews in 1872. Dodge City quickly became the biggest cattle shipping town in the west. It was equally famous for its saloons and dance halls and for the brawls and shoot-outs that were so common in the wild and woolly west.

Dodge City's peace officers included Wyatt Earp and Bat Masterson, and there were so many shootings there that the town set aside a plot of land not far from Front Street where men who died with their boots on could be buried without ceremony. The graveyard was called Boot Hill Cemetery and although many western towns have burial grounds of the same name, Dodge City claims to have had the first.

Dodge City's prominence as a cowtown came to an end in 1884 when the government forbade the importation of Longhorns from Texas to prevent the spread of a cattle disease called Texas Fever. Farming took over as the principal industry, but on the Fourth of July, 1884, there was one last roundup. It included, as part of the festivities, the first and only bullfight ever held in the United States. The event was touted so widely that state and federal authorities wired Mayor A.B. Webster to inform him that bullfighting was outlawed in the United States. With typical old West indifference to such matters, Webster wired back: "Dodge City is not in the U.S."

Four fires during the 1880's destroyed most of the original structures in Dodge City. Today the oldest building in town is a bank that opened in 1886. In the past few years, many of the buildings along Front Street have been replaced, and visitors can now stop in at the Longbranch Saloon, buy a sarsaparilla and listen to the player piano thumping out tunes of the 1870's. Boot Hill Museum at the foot of old Boot Hill Cemetery has a collection of old guns, and the graveyard behind it has some of the original tombstones. One epitaph says:

Jack Wagner killed Ed Masterson
April 9, 1878
Killed by Bat Masterson, April 9, 1878
He argued with the wrong man's brother.

In driving across the country, not many travelers think to stop at tiny Gardner, Kansas, but in many ways it is the most historic point on U.S. 50. It was here that two crudely lettered signs marked the way west. One pointing right said "Road to Oregon"; the other pointing left said "Road to Santa Fe." Emigrants by the thousands passed this crossroad in the days of America's great push toward the Pacific coast. Although few people today have ever heard of Gardner, it can justly be considered the place where our western highways began.

10

U.S. 30 The Oregon Trail

THE OREGON TRAIL

U.S. 30 has several claims to fame. One section of it is the old Lincoln Highway, America's first cross-country automobile road. Another section follows two even more famous roads—the Mormon Trail and the Oregon Trail.

Like most of America's highways, the road to Oregon evolved slowly. It had its beginnings in the trail followed by Meriwether Lewis and William Clark when they became the first white men to travel overland to the Pacific Ocean.

Lewis and Clark made their way up the Missouri River to its headwaters in the Rocky Mountains. From there they followed the Snake and Columbia Rivers downstream to the Pacific Ocean. U.S. 30 also follows the Snake and Columbia Rivers, but instead of taking Lewis and Clark's northern route through Montana and the Dakotas, it cuts across Wyoming and passes within fifty miles of the South Pass, an opening in the Rocky Mountains that was the route of the first travelers to Oregon.

South Pass was discovered by fur traders traveling back and forth to Astoria at the mouth of the Columbia River in Oregon. The city, the last stop on the Oregon Trail, was founded in 1811 by agents of John Jacob Astor's Pacific Fur Company, who reached the Pacific coast by sailing around the southern tip of South America.

A year after the trading post was established, one of the Astorians, Robert Stuart, took the land route back to the east. He is credited with being the first white man to use the South Pass. Two other fur traders later made the same trip—Captain Benjamin de Bonneville in 1832 and Captain Nathaniel Wyeth in 1836.

The next travelers to Oregon were missionaries. They came at the request of four Indians from the Flathead tribe, who arrived in St. Louis in 1831 asking for religious instruction for their people. The Flatheads had heard that the white man's religion included miraculous medicines and they wanted to learn more about them. In response to the Indians' plea, a number of missionaries soon arrived in Oregon. Among them were a Congregationalist minister, Dr. Marcus Whitman, and a Jesuit priest, Father Pierre Jean de Smet. Dr. Whitman came with his new bride, a lively young lady named Narcissa. She and another missionary's wife, Eliza Spaulding, became the first white women to cross the South Pass of the Rockies.

The journals of Lewis and Clark and Robert Stuart aroused a great deal of public interest in the Pacific Northwest. Two books by Washington Irving, *Astoria* and *The Adventures of Captain Bonneville,* were also widely read; but the book that attracted the most emigrants to Oregon was the account of an expedition made by Lieutenant John C. Fremont of the army's Topographical Corps.

Fremont's father-in-law, Senator Thomas Hart Benton of Missouri, was devoted to the idea of westward expansion, but he knew that many easterners were afraid to move west. They had heard too many tales of hazardous mountain passages, hostile Indians and unmarked trails. To allay their fears, Benton arranged for John Fremont to map out the Oregon Trail and issue a report on his travels to the Pacific Coast.

The twenty-nine-year-old officer set out for Oregon in the summer of 1842 with Kit Carson as his guide. He returned four months later, and with the help of his wife, Benton's daughter Jessie, wrote a sparkling account of his adventures. Fremont made the trip sound both easy and exciting. His report was read by thousands of Americans who immediately began making plans to come to Oregon.

The great migration began in the spring of 1843. Dr. Marcus Whitman, who had been in Boston on church business, returned

Major General John C. Fremont. (Culver Pictures)

with the first wagon train. There were a hundred and twenty wagons and over a thousand people in the group.

In many cities prospective settlers formed emigration societies to make the trip west. Sometimes they hired guides to accompany them. Sometimes they simply bought one of the dozens of guidebooks that appeared on the market. Not all of the books were reliable. Many of them made the cross-country trek sound as if it were no more than a long walk. More than a few would-be emigrants foolishly believed them and set out on foot alone and with no provisions. Almost all of them died of starvation or exhaustion before they reached the Pacific Coast. More prudent travelers joined a wagon train. For many years, the trains left at such regular intervals that there was often less than a thousand yards between them.

The eastern terminus of U.S. 30 is in New Jersey, but the section that follows the Oregon Trail starts in Omaha, Nebraska. From there it passes through most of the major stops on the original trail.

The first stop was Fort Laramie, where emigrants repaired their harnesses, rested their horses and tightened their wagon wheels for the long pull over the mountains. The present highway follows a gradual grade across the Rockies that was opened up by the transcontinental railroad, but the original trail crossed the mountains at South Pass. On the western slope of the Rockies, the journey became more tedious. The country was dry and barren, and the horses and mules often dropped in their tracks from exhaustion and thirst. The emigrants eventually learned to use oxen, which were slower but had far more endurance.

The first stop in Idaho was Fort Hall, near the present city of Pocatello. The fort was founded by Nathaniel Wyeth in 1834. "Having done as much as was requisite for safety to the fort and drank a bale of liquor and named it Fort Hall in honor of the oldest partner of our concern, we left it and with it Mr. Evans in charge of eleven men and fourteen horses and mules and three cows," Wyeth wrote in his journal. Just beyond Fort Hall, travelers to California left the Oregon Trail and struck out across northern Nevada.

Fort Boise, on the site of Idaho's present capital, Boise, was the second landmark in Idaho. After that came The Dalles in Oregon. By the time they reached The Dalles, many of the emigrants had run out of food. They were willing to trade almost anything for some rations of salt meat or fish. When the Jesuit missionary Father de Smet passed through here in the 1840's, he found the Indians wearing shoes and vests and one lucky brave—the envy of all his friends—sported a frilly white ladies' nightcap.

The Dalles was the site of Celilo Falls, the great falls of the Columbia River. For years the pioneers transferred their freight to canoes or barges here, lashed their wagons to rafts and sailed down the river to Fort Vancouver, opposite the present city of Portland.

The Columbia was one of several rivers along the road west. In Nebraska, the trail followed the Platte and the North Platte Rivers and in Idaho, the Snake River. The Snake, which William Clark originally named the Lewis in honor of his partner, forms 217 miles of the boundary between Idaho and Oregon. It flows through a steep gorge—deeper in some places than the Grand Canyon—that used to tantalize thirsty travelers on the Oregon Trail. Although the road ran right beside the river, it sometimes took several days to find a spot where they could climb down the rocky slopes and get a drink of water.

The long trail to Oregon was a test of human endurance and courage. The road was littered with castoff possessions—trunks and furniture that were simply too cumbersome to be carried any further. In many places crude gravestones still mark the burial places of emigrants who died along the way.

Some pioneers, however, found the journey a marvelous adventure. A Utah woman who traveled across the country around 1850 recalled the trip as a picnic. She and her brothers and sisters picked wildflowers and played hide and seek among the wagons. At night they sat with the adult members of the wagon train and sang or told stories around the campfire.

Other travelers were not so fortunate. The story is told of one couple, the Sagers, who started out from Oregon with their five

children. Both parents were stricken with cholera and died near Fort Hall, but the children, including a four-month-old baby, continued the journey by themselves. The oldest boy, John, who was fourteen, led them as far as Dr. Marcus Whitman's mission near Walla Walla, Washington. He appeared there carrying the

A wagon train resting at The Dalles. (Culver Pictures)

infant in his arms. His brother, Francis, was leading an emaciated cow with their two younger sisters, aged eight and five, clinging to its back. The children had walked a distance of five hundred miles, living on nothing but the cow's milk and whatever wild fruits they could find along the way.

Unfortunately, only two of the Sager youngsters survived. One of the girls, who had broken her leg on the trip, died soon after she arrived at the Whitman mission. The two boys, John and Francis, were killed three years later in an Indian attack on the mission in which both Dr. Whitman and his wife, Narcissa, also died.

The Whitman massacre was the result of a dispute between the missionaries and the Indians they had come to convert. In most instances, however, the Indians welcomed the white men to the northwest. They were curious about their clothes and their customs and fascinated by the trinkets and gadgets they carried in their wagons.

By the 1860's, the redmen's attitude had changed. They saw their lands being taken away from them and converted into white men's farms and cities. They were pushed onto reservations. Their deer and buffalo were killed and they were often left without enough food to live on. Not surprisingly, the Indians soon became determined to drive the intruders from their territory. They began attacking the white men every time they had the chance.

In the summer of 1862, a train of eleven wagons carrying twenty families from Iowa was ambushed at Massacre Rocks, near American Falls, Idaho. Nine of the emigrants were killed and many more were injured; their wagons were robbed, then set on fire, and the oxen were driven off.

Three years later a train of seventy-five wagons was attacked near Rock Creek, Wyoming. The Indians captured two little girls, Mary and Lizzie Fletcher. Mary, who was thirteen, managed to escape when her captors came to a white trading post, but her two-year-old sister remained behind. Thirty-five years later, a white woman was found living among the Indians on the Wind River Reservation, not far from the Oregon Trail. She was married to an Indian, John Brokenhorn, and spoke only Arapaho. Mary Fletcher heard the story, came to the reservation and identified the squaw as her sister Lizzie, but when Mary asked her to return to the white man's world, Lizzie refused. The reservation was her home and the Arapahoes had become her people.

Just beyond Rock Springs, Wyoming, Route 30 divides for a time into two separate highways, 30N and 30S. The former goes directly north into Idaho while the latter goes southwest across the Wasatch Mountains to Salt Lake City. This is the trail followed by the Mormons when they first came to Utah in 1847.

The sect had been driven out of their previous homes in Missouri and Illinois. When their founder, Joseph Smith, was murdered, Brigham Young became the new leader and in 1846 led them across the Mississippi River in search of a new home. The Mormons camped that winter in Omaha, Nebraska. Six hundred of them died before spring and are buried in the Mormon Cemetery there. In April the 143 men, three women and two children who survived, started west along the Oregon Trail. They went as far as Fort Laramie and then turned south toward Fort Bridger, a fur trading post that had been founded by a woodsman named Jim Bridger. From there they continued southwest through the Wasatch Mountains until they reached the valley of the Great Salt Lake. They arrived on July 24, 1847. Several more companies came later that same year and the Mormons built a thriving settlement.

By 1855 some 60,000 people had followed the Mormon Trail into Utah. Many of them, converts to Mormonism, came from England. One particularly large company had no money to buy wagons so they walked, pushing their children and possessions ahead of them in two-wheeled carts. By the time the Handcart Expedition arrived in Salt Lake City, many of its members had starved or frozen to death.

Occasionally travelers along the Oregon Trail stopped before they reached its end. The lands along the way were ideal for raising cattle, and a string of cowtowns soon sprouted along the route. Some, like North Platte, Nebraska, are still famous for their livestock.

Other towns grew up around the forts the United States government built to protect the travelers on the trail. Kearney, Nebraska, for instance, was once Fort Kearny (but no one knows how the final "e" got lost—or found) and Laramie and Boise are both close to the sites of the forts of the same name.

The town of Shelton, Nebraska, was founded when a party of Mormons from England led by Edward Oliver suffered a broken axle on their wagon. Unable to continue their journey, the family camped along the road for the winter and eventually decided to stay there. Oliver built a store, and the community that grew up around it was named Shelton after another settler, Nathaniel Shelton.

The Union Pacific Railroad helped build many of the towns along U.S. 30. Cheyenne, Wyoming's capital and largest city, had its first settlers in July 1867. By the time the tracks were laid the following November, 4000 people were living there.

Most of the settlers who came to the west were farmers or ranchers, but a few followed less respectable callings. Outlaws were a perpetual problem in the new territories. It was easier for a fugitive to elude the forces of law and order in the west than it was back east. Moreover, there were plenty of opportunities to earn a dishonest, as well as an honest, living. Stagecoaches and later trains could be waylaid, saloons and gambling houses robbed and rich cattle ranchers relieved of their herds.

The citizens of the west became their own lawmen and in many places developed a reputation for being as fearsome as the thieves they hunted down. In Rawlins, Wyoming, a group of vigilantes hanged a train robber in 1878 and then sent warning letters to twenty-four other outlaws who lived nearby. The next morning, the stationmaster at the Rawlins depot sold exactly twenty-four tickets on trains heading out of town.

Not all of the western outlaws were tough desperados; many were smooth-talking swindlers who gave the impression of being law-abiding citizens. At Diamond Mesa, near the town of Table Rock, Wyoming, a pair of prospectors once reported uncovering a staggering collection of diamonds, emeralds and other precious stones. The two made the story of their discovery sound so convincing that they persuaded a group of New York businessmen, including the newspaper editor, Horace Greeley, to invest more than half a million dollars in a company that would develop the gem mines. The money was half spent before the unhappy investors discovered that they were the victims of a hoax. The two prospectors had actually put the stones on Diamond Mesa themselves.

Like many of America's roads, the trail to Oregon declined in use after the coming of the railroad. Then in 1912, an Indianapolis businessman, Carl G. Fisher, conceived the idea of a coast-to-coast highway. Automobiles were still a novelty at the time, but Fisher contributed $1000 to the project himself and persuaded the leaders of the fledgling automobile companies to raise more than four million dollars more.

In 1913 Fisher formed the Lincoln Highway Association and began soliciting contributions from state legislatures and private citizens all over the country. A group of cement manufacturers donated the materials to build a few "demonstration miles" of highway, but the road was far from complete when the first automobiles set out on it on May 15, 1915. They found less than a hundred miles of concrete and macadam. The rest was gravel or mud and occasionally nothing more than cattle tracks.

The 3389-mile route started in Jersey City and passed through Philadelphia, Gettysburg, Pittsburgh, Fort Wayne, Omaha, Cheyenne, Salt Lake City, Sacramento and San Francisco. Averaging about twenty miles an hour and driving about ten hours a day, the fourteen drivers who made that first transcontinental trip took 104 days to reach San Francisco.

The Lincoln Highway was a great improvement over the old Oregon Trail, but now it, too, is obsolete. Both the highway and its counterpart, U.S. 30, are being replaced by a broad superhighway, Interstate 80. Similar interstate highways, the newest step in the development of America's roads, are being laid out all over the country. To avoid confusion with the old highway system, the numbering begins in the west and south instead of the east and north. The odd numbers still run from north to south and the evens from east to west.

No matter what name or number modern road builders give the Oregon Trail, they can never erase its links with the past. Fort Laramie has been restored and refurnished and is now a national historic site, and in Julia Davis Park in Boise there are several interesting old cabins. One, the Coston Cabin, which dates back to 1863, is made of driftwood gathered along the Boise River by pioneers and put together with pegs. The O'Farrell Cabin, built around the same time, was the first house in Boise to shelter women and children.

In some places the ruts worn by the wheels of the wagon trains are still faintly visible in the earth. Elsewhere, Oregon Trail markers point the way. The markers can be found in many towns along U.S. 30 and on nearby routes as well because, unlike concrete highways, early roads never followed an exact route. Travelers altered their course when a new trading post was built, a spring dried up or a watering place became polluted.

In Portland, the Oregon Historical Society has many maps and diaries of the state's first settlers. A monument to Lewis and Clark stands in Washington Park, and in Esther Short Park, there is a bronze statue of a pioneer woman, flintlock in hand, her children at her side. The woman, Esther Short, not only made the trip to Oregon but gave birth to a child along the way. When she and her husband built their first cabin in Portland, employees of the Hudson's Bay Fur Company tried to tear it down. Esther Short slapped one of the men so hard that they all fled and never bothered the Shorts again.

The Hudson's Bay Company, a competitor of John Jacob Astor's Pacific Fur Company, had its headquarters on the opposite side of the Columbia River in Vancouver. Dr. John McLoughlin, chief factor of the Company's Columbia District for over twenty years, was one of the most influential men in Oregon. It was he who planted the first apple trees in the Northwest.

At a dinner party in Portland in 1826, a British army officer, Captain Aemilius Simpson, took a handful of apple seeds from his pocket and laughingly remarked that a young woman whom he had met at a farewell party in London had asked him to plant them in the wilderness. McLoughlin, who was also present, saw nothing amusing about the request and insisted on planting the seeds and nurturing them into saplings. They became the first cultivated fruit trees in Oregon, a state now famous for its orchards.

Astoria marks the end of U.S. 30, just as it marked the end of the Oregon Trail. The Astoria Column on Coxcomb Hill, erected in 1926 by the great-grandson of John Jacob Astor, tells the story of the first settlement there. Five miles southwest of Astoria is Fort Clatsop National Memorial. It stands on the site where Meriwether Lewis and William Clark ended their journey to the Pacific Northwest. They camped there during the winter of 1805 when they became the first of millions of Americans to reach the western shores of the nation.

Index